The Reflecting Pond

The REFLECTING POND

MEDITATIONS FOR SELF-DISCOVERY

Liane Cordes

A Harper/Hazelden Book

Harper & Row, Publishers, San Francisco

Cambridge, Hagerstown, New York, Philadelphia, Washington
London, Mexico City, São Paulo, Singapore, Sydney

First Harper & Row edition published in 1988.

ISBN: 0-06-255475-1

88 89 90 91 92 HAZ 10 9 8 7 6 5 4 3 2 1

Contents

Chapter 1

Self-Acceptance and Self-Knowledge

"No man is born into the world whose work is not born with him."

—James Russell Lowell

Our Wise Creator has provided each of us, at birth, with the necessary talents and gifts to make a worthwhile contribution to the world. What we make of those gifts and talents is entirely up to us. We can choose to ignore, and thereby destroy, our innate interests and abilities—or we can choose to pursue them, despite our doubts and fears, and enjoy life to the fullest.

If we wish to use our talents and gifts, we must become aware of those activities and interests we enjoy. Then we must make the effort to explore the opportunities and alternatives available to us. If we do not find a place for our interests and abilities in the world around us, we needn't be discouraged. We can create one. Dedication and perseverance have opened many seemingly closed doors.

TODAY Am I doing the best with what I've been given? Am I using my capabilities well? If I am not, am I willing to take the necessary action to achieve inner satisfaction?

"One of the best ways I know to get in touch with myself, " a woman explained, "is to write my thoughts and feelings. When I express my reactions to the happenings of life—in the privacy of a journal—I can more easily sort out and work through my positive and negative feelings. A journal is a great tool for self-knowledge. And I don't have to be a 'great writer' to have it work. All I have to have is an earnest desire to know myself.

"You know, I've often surprised myself with my own insight and commonsense solutions to seemingly hopeless situations. And all I did was take time to clarify my thoughts by writing them down. It's wonderful to discover my deepest feelings and values. It's even greater to share my thoughts after they're clear in my own mind. Not only do I benefit from journal writing, but all my loved ones do, too!"

TODAY I will take time to get to know myself by putting my thoughts and feelings on paper. Clarifying my attitudes and reactions will help me share my concerns with others more calmly and serenely. I will also get a better perspective of myself and my experiences.

> "We can be redeemed only to the extent to which we see ourselves."
>
> —Martin Buber

God, grant me the serenity
To accept the things I cannot change
Courage to change the things I can
And wisdom to know the difference.

This well-known prayer expresses some key guidelines to our philosophy of living. One group member explained it this way:

"For me, the things I cannot change are other people, places, and circumstances. The only things I **can** change are my attitudes, reactions and actions toward the people, places and circumstances in my life.

"The wisdom to know the difference, well, that's a hard one. I don't always know what I can and cannot change until I try changing it. Wisdom comes by trial and error. The more experience I have, the more understanding, knowledge, and wisdom I have."

TODAY I will accept that much of my wisdom can only come through my daily experiences. I need to expect to make some mistakes in my attitudes, actions, and judgments of what I can and cannot change. I will learn to be patient with myself and others as I gain more understanding from my mistakes.

Letting parents, relatives, spouses, church members, peers, or friends do our thinking for us leads to total confusion and helplessness. We neither allow God to speak to us nor do we come face to face with ourselves.

A member explained it this way: "After trying to do, say, and think what other people told me was right, I ran the other way for a number of years. But one day, in a state of total despair, I heard God say to me, 'Are you ready to listen to Me now?'

"By looking inside myself, and really examining the way I felt, I got in touch with God and myself. I discovered many of the things that are right and good for me that God has written in all our hearts.

"Now by **listening** to my inner voice—call it conscience, God, what you will—and by **obeying** what I hear, I have a peace of mind I never had before."

TODAY I affirm that my inner voice (God within me) will tell me what I need to hear if I listen. I will cling tightly to my faith, and I will do what I know is right for me.

"I should be perfect." "I should be competent." "I should be responsible." "I should put others first."

How many of these "should's" govern our lives? How many unrealistic expectations do we have of ourselves? How many of us condemn ourselves because we don't measure up to what we think, or were taught to think, we "should" be? Let's examine these expectations in the light of our own experiences.

Perfection and competence are worthwhile goals. It is the striving for them that has given us joy, and we have all had to make mistakes in order to expand our knowledge, wisdom, and skills. Perfection and competence have not been gained without error or additional education and insight.

Similarly, responsibility and putting others first are worthwhile traits. But those of us who have had the courage to try it know from experience that we are most responsible to others when we are most responsible to ourselves. Before we can be responsible to others, we must first learn to be accountable to ourselves!

TODAY I will not have unrealistic expectations of myself. I will allow myself to make mistakes, for that is the way I learn and grow toward perfection. I will realize I am most responsible to others when I am true to my deepest convictions and values.

Every trial and frustration in our lives is an opportunity to expand our self-awareness and rise above our current limitations. Attempting to avoid any unpleasantness or suffering in our lives prevents us from growing and leaves us bitterly unprepared for—and dreading—any unpredictable event that may occur.

To expect the universe, our jobs, or our relationships to run without friction is contrary to all the laws of nature. Just as nature has its turmoil in thunderstorms and earthquakes, we have our internal upheavals and conflicting pressures. Just as trees require pruning to bear more fruit, we need old ideas removed so that we may grow and prosper.

TODAY I will use any discomfort or tension I feel as an instrument of growth. I will learn something new about myself and the laws which govern my nature.

> "The gem cannot be polished without
> friction, nor man perfected without trials."
>
> —Confucius

If we are weighed down by difficulties for which we have no workable solutions, we will be powerless to help others who have similar problems. We cannot expect satisfactory help from those who have limitations similar to our own. The best we can usually do under such circumstances is to identify and share our common limitations and pain.

To rid ourselves of pressing questions or frustrations, we must find others who have not only experienced, but **overcome,** our particular problem. Sharing a burdened heart with another, who has the wisdom, strength, and knowledge to carry it, frees us from its weight long enough to focus on solutions.

TODAY I realize I cannot help others effectively until I help myself. I will admit I need help from someone wiser and stronger than I, no matter how much it hurts my pride. I will be open to that person's suggestions.

"No laden soul can bear another's burdens."

—Holy Koran

"And if the blind lead the blind, both
shall fall into the ditch."

—Matthew 15 : 14

Am I apathetic, indifferent to the opportunities before me? Do I continually refuse to act on what I know is right?

We are all familiar with the compulsive personality that grasps at anything and everything in hope of satisfaction. Such personalities over-do everything; they drink, talk, entertain, work, play, and take unnecessary risks to excess.

Yet, there is another type of behavior just as suicidal. We might call these people "the living dead." Largely passive, they are afraid of rejection or ridicule and thus do not grasp life's opportunities. They slip into inertia, with little energy to do anything. Constant fatigue, boredom, disinterest, and blandness characterize their response to life.

TODAY I will realize that self-destructive behavior comes in many forms. Do I always do everything to excess? Am I threatened by others? Do I find few things interesting? An affirmative answer to any of these questions shows me I need to make some serious changes in my attitudes and actions if I want to have a full and productive life.

Whether we realize it or not, many of us are fulfilling the Commandment, "Love thy neighbor as thyself." We cannot give love to others if we do not love ourselves.

If we are filled with self-doubt, we will be suspicious of our neighbors; if we see only the negatives in ourselves, we will be equally critical of our neighbors; if we hold on to past hurts and fears, we will expect others to hurt us—and we will regard them with fear.

If, on the other hand, we accept our imperfections, we can be more tolerant of others; if we make our own decisions, we can respect others' choices; and if we forgive those who have caused us pain, we can help others to overcome their bitterness and sorrow.

TODAY I will work on accepting and loving myself just as I am. I will make a conscious effort to accept and love others just as they are. For it is only by accepting myself for what I am that I may discover what I may become.

> "Nothing is a greater impediment to being on good terms with others than being ill at ease with yourself."
>
> —Balzac

The keys to constructive self-awareness are observation, admission, and examination. First, we must observe ourselves as objectively as possible. Second, we admit what we see. Third, we examine the possible causes of our reactions and actions.

If we experience boredom in solitude, for instance, we try not to judge or condemn ourselves. We simply admit our boredom. Examining its cause, we may find we are not living up to our fullest potential or that we depend too much on others for entertainment.

If we experience a sense of futility or uselessness, we admit that, too. Probing the source of our emptiness, we may discover we have based our self-worth solely on helping others or on producing tangible results. We may have neglected the "being" part of our natures in favor of "doing" and "having."

TODAY I will make time to get to know myself. I will observe my reactions, admit my feelings, and examine their cause. Only then will I discover what I wish to change in myself.

". . .let us examine our own hearts and see that they are right before we criticize or condemn our neighbors."

—Ida Scott Taylor

"When I'm depressed," a friend confided, "I become a stranger to myself. Nothing seems important to me. I lose interest in the things I once valued and enjoyed. What's wrong with me?"

For many of us, depression is an ugly word and a frightening experience. We try to avoid it at all costs. In attempting to run away from our lows, we often seek escape in food, sex, drugs, sleep, work and play. Yet, despite our frantic efforts, despair engulfs us and we wonder what is wrong with us. Sometimes we are so overwhelmed with a sense of failure that we don't learn from depression.

Depressions are not disasters. Ebbs in our spirits are as natural as floods of joy. Without the constant ebb and flow of the tides, we would not have the ocean's beauty or nourishment; we'd have a stagnant, worldwide sewer.

Once we learn to welcome our lows as part of the natural order of things, we can begin to learn from even our deepest sorrows and trials.

TODAY I will not try to run away from my low moods. I will seek the cause of my pain so that I will have a better understanding of myself and the laws which govern my nature.

Chapter 2

Anger and Fear

Fear of rejection or disapproval may keep me from taking the risks necessary for personal growth. I can choose to let fear paralyze me, or I can choose to take a risk and expand my horizons.

If I want to expand my horizons, I must be willing to make mistakes. I must realize that I won't get what I want without taking action.

If I feel an attraction towards someone I've recently met, I can let my fear cause me to withdraw or I can reach out, in spite of my fear, and learn something about myself and the way I interact with others. Even if a friendship doesn't develop, I have made a giant step in overcoming my fear of other people.

TODAY I will take the action necessary for my personal growth, even if it frightens me. I will gain new insight no matter what the outcome may be.

> "Seems to me that the highest possible reward for any man's labor is not what he gets for it, but what he becomes by it."
>
> —Brock Bell

How many of us, before our exposure to this living philosophy, were afraid to take charge of our lives? How many of us sought to compensate for our fears of inadequacy by assuming others' responsibilities and problems?

Once we accept this philosophy of living and begin practicing it in all our affairs, we find we are no longer slaves to our frustration, anger, and fear. We no longer need another's dependence on us to achieve a sense of self-worth, and our moods are not at the whim of someone else's discomfort or self-doubt.

We are shown how to overcome our difficulties by limiting our concerns to things we can handle. We are told to live one day at a time. We are reminded we can change no one but ourselves. We are advised to work in partnership with God—not play God. We are encouraged to be good to ourselves. For the first time in our lives, we are freed from our dependencies and given support to become the people we were meant to be.

TODAY I am grateful for all I am learning and have learned. I am thankful for my new freedom and for my new sense of faith in myself and God.

As long as fear dominates our thinking we can do little to change our circumstances for the better. Fear paralyzes any useful or constructive action. Fears of defeat, humiliation, danger, inadequacy, and suffering drain our strength and courage to face the challenges of life. Our fears also prevent us from pursuing opportunities for growth and success. In fact, fear often creates the very situations we dread.

To change this self-destructive pattern, we must replace our negative outlooks with positive ones. One way to do this is to deliberately voice a life-giving thought for every life-draining thought that crosses our minds. At the beginning, we would be wise to repeat this uplifting phrase ten to fifteen times a day until it is solidly lodged in our minds. Many of us have found Biblical quotations (i.e., "If God be for us, who can be against us?" or "I can do all things through God Who strengthens me,") a great help in curing fear and despair.

TODAY I will replace an inspiring thought for every fear-filled thought I have. I will repeat that positive thought until my fear goes and my strength and faith are renewed.

> ". . .the only thing we have to fear is fear itself—nameless, unreasoning, unjustified terror which paralyzes needed efforts to convert retreat into advance."
>
> —Franklin D. Roosevelt

Do I rarely try something new? Do I avoid sharing my thoughts and feelings with others? Do I have difficulty making decisions?

If the answer to any of these questions is "yes," I may be limiting my progress and growth. If I am continually trying to control my natural inclinations, I may never develop or express the abilities I have.

Change and growth can only come from taking risks. When we place ourselves in difficult or challenging situations we discover what is hidden within.

This does not mean, of course, that we should rush headlong into some death-defying activity to show off or get a personal "high" for momentary pleasure. Taking risks means being willing to face uncertainty. We minimize our "risks" by developing our abilities and by gaining the knowledge we need to succeed.

TODAY I will not let my fear limit my growth. I will set myself a goal, assess my progress daily, and not stop my efforts until I feel the satisfaction of accomplishing my goal.

Setting goals helps me overcome my fear of loneliness and rejection. Working toward these goals directs my energies into meaningful activities and minimizes my tendency to rely too heavily on others' opinions, advice, or support for my sense of self-worth.

It does not matter what kind of goal I set. What matters is that I give myself the necessary time and make the necessary efforts to reach it.

If setbacks occur, I merely begin again **after** analyzing the cause of my failure. Did I lack a certain skill? Did I let fear of making a mistake immobilize me? Was I paralyzed by self-doubt? Do I need more information and understanding? Did I try too hard or become too impatient? As soon as I discover the cause, I will work toward eliminating it by gaining new perspective, knowledge, or skill. As I improve myself, I will move closer to my goal on my next try.

TODAY I will learn new things about myself by setting worthwhile goals. I will work on achieving these goals **one day at a time.** I will use setbacks to increase my present skills, education, and self-knowledge.

Alcoholism and chronic ill-health, drug abuse and child abuse, over-eating and over-extending ourselves are all symptoms of deeper problems. They are merely the external effects of our inner "diseases." Uncomfortable with ourselves and our thoughts, we often inflict pain on ourselves, our loved ones, and complete strangers.

Since our fears are the primary cause of our discomfort, it would be wise to examine them if we want to rid ourselves of destructive impulses.

Do we fear rejection or ridicule? Do we fear success or failure? Do we fear our inadequacy? Do we feel that others will control us? Do we fear honesty and intimacy? Do we fear pain or "weakness"?

Once we examine, not resist, our inner fears, once we admit our actions and attitudes might be irrational, we can then replace our destructive attitudes with constructive ones.

TODAY I know my addictive compulsions are only the outward expressions of my inner thoughts. If I replace harmful thinking habits with healthy ones, I will no longer be at the mercy of disease, despair, and abuse.

Indecision cripples constructive action and destroys peace of mind. Indecision is also a refusal to shoulder our share of the responsibility for our own lives and leads to unhealthy dependence on other people's acceptance and direction for our sense of self-esteem and meaning.

Evading an issue, by refusing to make a decision, never solves anything. It only keeps us in a state of helplessness, despair, and fear.

To take control of our lives, we need to practice the habit of making decisions. Not all of our decisions will be correct; none of us is perfect. But as we live out the consequences of our best judgment, we will develop the experience and wisdom to make better choices. What is more, we will get something done and be less resentful or influenced by other people's attitudes, abilities, and opinions.

TODAY I will not fear making a decision. I will view all sides to a question or problem bothering me, and then I will take constructive action.

> "Indecision is fatal. It is better to make a wrong decision than build up a habit of indecision.
>
> —Marie Beynon Ray

In 1914, Dr. Walter Cannon concluded that the refusal to deal with anger and fear can trigger physical illness. More recently, Dr. Meyer Friedman and Dr. Carl Simonton found that tensions and frustrations resulting from overwhelming, yet ignored, feelings of anger, guilt, and fear lower our immunizational system and allow harmful bacteria to trigger disease. Among the psychosomatic diseases described by these two physicians are heart trouble, cancer, ulcers, arthritis, asthma, and colds.

Physical illness is often the body's way of indicating the presence of destructive emotions. Often, we are not even conscious of our harmful attitudes until we face a physical crisis or collapse.

When we have the courage to take responsibility for our suffering, and ask ourselves and our doctors how we have helped create our distress, we are on the road to recovery and health.

TODAY I will not ignore feelings of anger, guilt, or fear. I will share them with a trusted friend before their effects cripple my health. I will seek a better understanding of myself and others through honest and open discussion.

> "It is clear that every illness and every accident reveal problems, sometimes of vital importance, in which physical, psychological, and spiritual factors are closely interwoven."
>
> —Paul Tournier, M.D.

To compensate for inadequate self-images, many of us adopt an unhealthy "I'll Show You!" attitude. In this frame of mind, we regard everyone and everything in our lives as a potential threat to our survival and self-worth. Life becomes a continual battleground in which someone must "win" and someone must "lose." We employ every war-like strategy we know to be the "victors" in the battle.

In verbal exchanges, we make sure to get the last word, or we batter away at our adversary's weakest points. We "win" by intimidation or by vindictive, cold silence. If we feel we have "lost" the battle, we retreat but still harbor thoughts of revenge or hate. Some of us may even wait patiently for another chance to "get even." And so the vicious war continues. The more we try to prove or justify ourselves, the more we prolong our turmoil and anger and increase our despair and pain. No one "wins" and everyone suffers.

TODAY I will see life as a conquest over myself, not others.

> "Though a man go out to battle a thousand times against a thousand men, if he conquers himself he is the greater conqueror."
>
> —Buddhist Proverb

Continually getting angry at the circumstances or people in our lives never solves anything. Out of control emotions only make matters worse. We inflict pain on ourselves and the people around us when we impulsively respond out of anger, fear, or self-pity. In that frame of mind, we tend to attack others because we feel everything that happens to us is an intentional insult or a direct attack against us.

All of us face setbacks in our lives. But we can prevent them from becoming insurmountable crises by responding calmly. After all, the majority of unfortunate experiences we face are not threats to our safety or our lives if we have founded our inner security on something more powerful than others' opinions or outward circumstances.

TODAY I will re-examine my old values in the light of any discontentment I may experience. I will make sure I have not made gods of other people's approval nor depended too much on material things as the basis of my security.

> "Anger is often a substitute for knowledge; violence, a defense against truth."
>
> —Dr. William Arthur Ward

Chapter 3

Worry and Stress

A study of case histories by a group of physicians has found that **worry** is the greatest cause of illness. According to this study, our worries fall into three categories: 40% concern the past, 50% are about the future, and 10% are about our present difficulties.

Worry is a habit we have acquired and must eliminate if we want peace of mind and body. Many of us know from experience that anxiety over matters we can do nothing about today often results in fatigue, depression, backaches, and upset stomachs. Some of us have even experienced the more drastic effects of heart or cancer problems.

TODAY I will live only One Day At A Time. I will remind myself that it is not what faces me today that makes me sick; rather, it is regret or bitterness for something which happened yesterday—and the fear of what tomorrow may bring—that makes me ill or drives me to despair.

> "Any man can fight the battles of just one day. It is only when we add the burdens of those two awful eternities—yesterday and tomorrow—that we break down."
>
> —Anonymous

"It seems most of my time and effort," a group member relates, "is spent dwelling on the past and re-living a lot of the unhappiness that was in my life. I'm constantly asking myself hundreds of confusing questions: Why wasn't I loved? Why couldn't I ever achieve? Why was I always put down? Why wasn't I ever good enough?

"Instead of living each day to the fullest, looking for the good things in my life each day, and doing things I, myself, enjoy doing, I rob myself of a lot of happiness I could be having today.

"True, these things did happen to me, even if I don't understand why. All I can do now is accept that they did happen and go on to Act II—being happy and getting the most out of my today."

TODAY ". . .I am still not all I should be, but I am bringing all my energies to bear on this one thing: Forgetting the past and looking forward to what lies ahead."

—TLB Philippians 3 : 13

"Wallowing in my woes only increases them. Self-pity saps my strength and courage and poisons any constructive action or thought."

"What if she leaves me?" "What if we can't pay our bills?" "What if I lose my job, my husband, my family?" "What IF. . . ?"

Although these can be very helpful questions in times of stress, when we **are** faced with these possibilities, some of us make a habit of worrying about future troubles that never occur. Some of us find a kind of martyr-like enjoyment in expecting the worst to happen every minute of our lives. And sometimes, the more we think about impending disaster, the more we actually create it in our lives.

If we are faced with a crisis today, we can take a long, calm look at our possible alternatives. Then we can act on the most suitable one. If, on the other hand, we are creating a crisis which does not exist yet, we are wasting our today and destroying our health in fruitless worry.

TODAY I will put my problems in their proper perspective by submitting each one to this test: Is there anything I can do about this today? If so, I will do it. If not, I will not waste my precious minutes worrying about it.

> "There is no use worrying about things over which you have no control, and if you have control, you can do something about them instead of worrying."
>
> —Stanley C. Allyn

We cannot stress too much the importance of living **one day at a time.** Since we cannot directly change what happened in the past, and since we cannot know in detail what will happen in the future, all we can have in our immediate control is what happens this moment in our lives.

We can choose to waste this precious moment by beating ourselves over the head for past mistakes, or we can choose to live this minute fully by reacting differently than we did before—with more patience, open-mindedness, and love. We can choose to be more vulnerable and less defensive; we can listen more than talk; we can learn rather than stagnate; we can reach out to others rather than withdraw.

These twenty-four hours are filled with unlimited possibilities if we concentrate on getting the most out of each minute as it comes. We can fill our minds with positive and productive thoughts, or we can wallow in self-pity and self-justification. The choice is entirely ours.

TODAY I will concentrate on growing one step at a time, **one day at a time.** If my mind begins to dwell on the past or dread the future too much, I will gently remind myself that I can live only one day at a time.

"Whatever this minute brings is sufficient for my needs and progress."

"Make plans but don't plan results." This is a simple phrase cautioning us against unnecessary worry and stress.

If our plans involve other people, we would be wise to work joyfully toward realizing our dreams, but we should not expect or worry if others do not want the same goals. Nor should we worry if others are not as enthused about our ideas as we are. We know, by applying the Serenity Prayer, that we can only change ourselves; we cannot force changes in others.

Another cause of unnecessary stress in planning results comes from our ingrained habit of regarding ourselves as inadequate. All too often, those of us who make plans give up on ourselves when we predict the outcome of our dreams on the basis of our past experiences. We falsely conclude that because we failed or felt empty in the past, we'll most certainly not succeed in the future; thus, we quit too soon and rationalize our resignation with a, "Why bother to try?" attitude.

TODAY I will make plans but not plan results. I will work out my plan, one day at a time, knowing that my past performance is NOT an infallible indicator of my present or future success. I will look forward with hope, not despair.

The word "sanity" is derived from the Latin word Sanitas which means "health." In our group, we think of health as wholeness of mind, body, and spirit.

One way to achieve health and wholeness is by living one day at a time. To do this successfully, we need to realize we cannot undo a single act we performed or unsay any harsh words spoken in the past. No matter how much we may regret or re-feel yesterday's painful experiences, there is nothing we can do to change what happened. The past is forever beyond our control.

The same thing is true of the future. No matter how much we may worry and fret over it, very few of us can predict what tomorrow will bring. We can only prepare for a hope-filled future by living fully and confidently today.

TODAY is all I have. Let me make the most of it.

> "You had better live your best and act your best and think your best today; for today is the sure preparation for tomorrow and all the other tomorrows that follow."
>
> —Harriet Martineau

> "Our grand business undoubtedly is not to see what lies dimly at a distance but to do what lies clearly at hand."
>
> —Thomas Carlyle

"All too often," confesses a gal, "I get so caught up in hurry and worry that I ignore my own needs. I push myself so hard to get this and that done that I make myself physically ill before I have the sense to rest. There's got to be a better way!"

Some of us, it seems, have to learn the importance of rest and relaxation the hard way. We push ourselves to the limit, often to the point of illness or injury, before we allow ourselves to stop.

We can avoid this vicious circle if we realize our limitations. One of those limitations is found in the law of "Supply and Demand." We cannot meet demands if we have depleted our resources. Just as a fire cannot burn without fuel, so our bodies and minds cannot function without food and rest.

TODAY—**before** I drive myself to the point of complete exhaustion, I will set aside as much time as I need to fill my depleted energies. I will get more rest, participate in an enjoyable activity, or have an inspiring conversation with a friend to renew my strength and courage.

"I'm learning it's what I do with my **today** that counts," said one group member. "I can make this a day to remember or a day to regret just by the kinds of thoughts I have about it."

"Let me explain what happened to make me realize this," he continued. "Two days ago, I woke up grumbling about my sorry lot in life. My divorce, my bills, and a recent argument with a close friend haunted me. Throughout the whole day I nursed my woes and convinced myself that this was just another rotten day. And do you know what? That's exactly what it turned out to be! Nothing went right. I even had a second argument with another friend who called to cheer me up.

"Yesterday, I overheard someone say that a person is made or unmade by what he thinks. I thought about this for a while and decided to try it out today. Instead of greeting the day with my usual, 'Good God, **morning!**' attitude, I consciously said, '**Good** morning, God!' with the expectation that it would be a good day. And that's what it's been. I even called my two friends to apologize for my previous terrible mood, and I had a warm and friendly conversation with them both!"

TODAY I will lift up my thoughts. In expecting nothing but good to come to me, that is exactly what I will receive.

When we first begin practicing these principles in our daily lives, we often become discouraged by expecting too much of ourselves. Then, when we don't meet our expectations, we are tempted to give up on ourselves and the very principles that can help us.

This is why it is so important to take one step at a time **at our own pace.** Just as we cannot force uninvited changes in others, we cannot force changes in ourselves that we are not ready to make. All we can do is practice these principles as best we can one day at a time. For some of us, this practice may only result in a daily, growing awareness—a broadening of our former thinking patterns. This, in itself, is a big step. It is only with our awareness of the need for change that constructive action can be taken. Awareness, then, is the first step necessary to prepare for change.

TODAY I will become more aware of my attitudes, actions, and reactions. I will remind myself, as I prepare for change, that acorns do not become oak trees overnight.

"It's the steady, constant driving
to the goal for which you're striving,
not the speed with which you travel,
that will make your victory sure. . ."

—Author Unknown

Chapter 4

Friendship and Love

Our choice of friends largely depends upon our priorities and needs.

If, for example, we have a desperate "need to be needed," we will pick friends who need "saving." If we prize popularity, we will attract similarly competitive and approval-seeking people. If we cherish self-honesty and learning, we will be drawn to others with similar interests and qualities. And if we are searching for faith, we will choose to surround ourselves with spiritually-minded friends.

Before we plunge into any new friendships, then, we would be wise to ask ourselves what we really want out of life. Do we want fun? Growth? Entertainment? Dependency? Change? Status? Security? Faith? Escape? Self-knowledge? Authority? Possessions? Honesty? Communication? Debates? Intimacy? Sexual gratification? Pity? Help? Enlightenment? Inspiration? Creativity?

Once we decide what is most important to us, we are better able to develop friendships which will help us achieve our goals.

TODAY I will examine my needs and priorities. I will actively seek friendships with those who can help me achieve my deepest desires

"There are times in my life when I need a push to get me going in the right direction," a fellow confessed. "That's why I'm grateful to have the friends I have.

"Sometimes, I get so down on myself, I can't do anything. I think I don't have anything to offer. Or I think I've made a mess out of my whole life.

"Expressing these feelings to a good friend gives me a better perspective. It's great to find out that my friends keep believing in me even when I don't believe in myself. I need their support and inspiration—just as they need mine.

"Friends help me overcome my self-doubt and inspire me to do my best. I hope I'm the kind of friend who gives the same encouragement and support in return."

TODAY I am grateful for my friends. I will strive to be as supportive, loyal, and caring of others as my friends are to me.

> "The glory of friendship is not the outstretched hand, nor the kindly smile, nor the joy of companionship. It is the spiritual inspiration that comes to one when he discovers that someone else believes in him and is willing to trust him."
>
> —Ralph Waldo Emerson

"You know," somebody admitted, "I've never really allowed myself to have good friends.

"I always put myself in two extreme roles. Either I think it's my duty to 'save' everyone, or I think it's someone else's function to 'save' me. I set myself up for very dissatisfactory relationships that way. I don't grow very much nor do the people I'm involved with grow much. We get locked into Parent-Child, Teacher-Student, Counselor-Client kinds of roles.

"I'm tired of empty and lopsided friendships. I want good friends, not parasites or Messiahs running my life. I want friends I can just be me with and not worry whether I'm one-up or one-down on them. I want friends who will accept me as I am and not expect me to have all the answers for all the questions all the time."

TODAY I will examine what I expect of myself and my friendships. As a friend, do I expect myself to give all the advice and have all the answers? Do I expect my friends to take care of me, and give me all the answers? If my friendships are not satisfactory, I will work on enlarging my concept of what a friend is. I will also work on improving the quality of my own friendship.

> "Treat your friends as you would a bank account—refrain from drawing too heavily on either."
>
> —Samuel Johnson

Friendships or marriages based on "dire need" or physical security are doomed to fail if each person in the relationship does not grow beyond his or her limited ways of thinking and reacting.

The ideal relationship is one in which each partner strives to grow. It is an ever-expanding commitment, mutually supportive of each person's need for change and growth. This is the secret of healthy interdependence: A healthy relationship encourages the seeking of wider mental and spiritual horizons; it is never threatened permanently by them.

TODAY Do I give my loved ones enough room to grow? Do I encourage my friends or mate to do things without me? Am I threatened by change or do I welcome it? Do I have the courage to do things on my own, even if my loved ones do not give me support? Do I have the courage and consideration to share my changes with those I love?

> "Let the purpose of all marriages and friendships alike be the deepening of the spirit and the enrichment of the soul."

Am I unloving if I seek self-fulfillment while my loved ones continue to suffer from self-doubt and despair? Do I have to react negatively or angrily just because others do?

None of us has to be the victim of another's attitude or reaction. Since each of us is given the gift of life to do with as we wish, each of us is free to choose those people or things which enhance rather than those which destroy peace of mind.

"Constant complainers," affirmed a member, "drag me down. I avoid them."

"I used to be with people who were continually involved in some crisis," said another. "That kind of tension drained me. Now I choose friends who want to grow and learn, not wallow."

Still another related, "My mate escapes in television and the newspaper. We never talk. So I go to lectures or read an inspiring book. I refuse to be imprisoned by someone else's fear and self-doubt."

TODAY I will be good to myself. I will seek out those people or activities which inspire me. I will not expect another, no matter how close to me, to share my sources of comfort and joy.

When I am offended or hurt by what someone says or does, it is vitally important to look at my own part in the unhappy incident. Only by examining my motives for my behavior and attitudes will I be free from the potentially damaging results of anger and resentment.

Was I sarcastic or self-centered? Discerning or demanding? Patient or impatient? Complaining or seeking new insight? Open-minded or inflexible? Attacking or listening? Resentful or loving? Self-righteous or uplifting?

By taking an honest look at my role in the conflict, often with the aid of a friend's welcome observations, I am better able to root out any self-deception regarding my real motives and reactions.

If I find I have helped create the offensive situation, I will make a special effort to apologize for my hurtful behavior. If I can find no fault in my actions or attitudes, I will still make a special effort to contact the offending person to show my continuing love for him or her.

TODAY I will build more bridges than walls. I will examine my own role in my conflicts, admit my shortcomings, and take the initiative to act on my growing awareness. I will not concern myself with how another responds to my amends or acts of love.

One source of loneliness is caused by too few friendships or not having enough quality friendships. In order to get a better perspective of our attitudes toward friendship, let us look at what others have said about it:

"All men have their frailties, and whoever looks for a friend without imperfections will never find what he seeks." —Cyrus

"Everyone yearns for friendship. But few want it badly enough to achieve as much of it as they yearn for. . .For friendship takes time. It takes time to achieve and time to maintain." —Norman Shidle

"A man with few friends is only half-developed; there are whole sides of his nature which are locked up and have never been expressed." —Randolph Bourne

"Friendships multiply joys, and divide griefs." —Henry Bohn

"Friendship is like a treasury; you cannot take from it more than you put into it." —Anonymous

"We do not make friends as we make houses but discover them as we do the arbutus, under the leaves of our lives, concealed in our experiences." —William Rader

TODAY Do I lack quality friends? Am I satisfied with the number of friends I have? Am I a good friend to others? I will make whatever efforts are necessary to change the loneliness in my life.

Do we expect our friends to sympathize with us? Do we want them to agree with us even if they think we are wrong? Do we seek friends who have the exact same interests we do? If we find ourselves saying "yes" to most of these questions, perhaps we had better take a second look at our friendships.

A true friend is one who has the courage to disagree with us when he or she thinks we are in error. A true friend will suggest alternate courses of action, or give positive direction, rather than allow us to wallow in our misery. A true friend will possess similar principles but he or she will also have different interpretations of those principles. Our friend may even express a different opinion regarding a shared event or experience. And, most certainly, a true friend will have other interests and concerns than we.Otherwise, we might never learn anything new from each other.

TODAY I will re-evaluate my concepts of friendship. I will change those attitudes in myself which limit my having quality friendships. I will seek equality and allow individual differences in all my relationships.

> "A true friend unbosoms freely, advises justly, assists readily, adventures boldly, takes all patiently, defends courageously, and continues a friend unchangeably."
>
> —William Penn

"God speaks to me through my friends," a gal commented. "The more I risk sharing with my friends, the more insight, trust, and wisdom I gain. Self-disclosure is a way for me to clarify my own thoughts. The very act of telling a friend what's in my mind and heart is an act of prayer for me.

"I don't mean the kind of sharing that's one-way—me talking and you only listening. I mean a two-way sharing in an honest, sincere, and encouraging atmosphere. I share openly with my friend and my friend shares back from his or her experience. It's a dialogue not a monologue.

"Talking with friends also widens my horizons. It takes me beyond a limited view of myself. To me, friendship is a source of spiritual inspiration. It's God's love made real."

TODAY I will remind myself of what John Ruskin said about friendship:

> "Friendship is the nearest thing we know to religion. God is love, and to make religion akin to friendship is simply to give it the highest expression conceivable to man."

Chapter 5

Disappointment and Frustration

"I used to think it was a catastrophe if everything didn't go my way," said a member. "I thought I knew what was best for everyone, including myself. I rarely delegated authority. If the job was to be done right, I had to do it."

"Well," she confessed, "I created a lot of heartache for myself with that attitude. Nothing and no one ever met my expectations. I was in constant turmoil, but I was too proud and scared to admit that I couldn't handle the mess I'd created. I made myself physically sick, and I finally collapsed from the strain.

"It was only after radical surgery that I realized that I couldn't carry the world on my shoulders. I was forced to ask for help.

"Since then I've learned I'm not God, that I don't have all the answers, and that it's not humiliating to ask for help."

TODAY I will admit weakness so I may become strong.

> "The man with insight enough to admit his limitations comes nearest to perfection."
>
> —Goethe

Many of us, whether we are conscious of it or not, create much of the unhappiness we experience. Our disappointments are the result of our own negative or limited thoughts about ourselves and our world. What are some of those limiting thoughts, those subconscious beliefs, which keep us from experiencing joy and wholeness?

One of those beliefs is that we cannot be fulfilled unless we are loved and accepted by those who are important to us: our parents, peers, children, bosses, spouses, or friends. Another false belief is that we are the victims of our past experiences, that we are "too old" or "too set in our ways" to change. Still another false idea is, "It's a catastrophe if things don't go my way!" Then, too, there's the self-defeating attitude that "to love is to lose, so I'd better prepare for the worst to happen because it will." Two more irrational beliefs are, "I have no control over my happiness" and "I want life to be easy and without hassles; therefore, I'll avoid discomfort or any new commitments."

TODAY I will see each disappointment in my life as a challenge to discover the negative or limited beliefs which keep me from seeing myself as a person of unlimited resources and potential.

Very few of us have gone through life without experiencing disappointment. We have not only disappointed ourselves but we have also been disappointed by others. In reacting to these hurts, we have all experienced feelings of self-pity, sorrow, revenge, resignation, denial, anger, frustration and intolerance. Many of us have impulsively acted on our initial hurt reaction to the detriment of ourselves and those around us—often alienating ourselves from ourselves as well as those we love most.

In our sense of helplessness, we blame others for causing our distress. We complain about being used or neglected. We accuse others of insensitivity to our needs. We take verbal or silent revenge. We condemn ourselves. We avoid the person who hurt us, or we busy ourselves so we don't have to think about our pain and its real source.

TODAY I will examine the real source of any disappointment I may feel. I will go beyond my initial response of anger or fear and ask myself, "What beliefs or values are being threatened, reaffirmed, or need to be expanded in order for me to be at peace with myself, others, and my circumstances?"

If we blindly accept someone else's beliefs or opinions—taking them as our own—then we set ourselves up for disappointment and heartache. If we do not examine another's viewpoint, in the light of our own experiences and abilities, we place the control of our happiness or sorrow in someone else's hands.

A gentleman illustrated this point with a story from his own life: "My father always regarded sticking with one job as a mark of stability. This, he felt, was emotional maturity. Even though he stayed unhappily at the same job for years, I never questioned his opinion.

"So, when I lost my first teaching job, I lost all my self-confidence as well as my father's approval. I believed I was emotionally immature and unstable. Then, after four more teaching job disasters, I discovered what the real issue was. It wasn't my lack of maturity or stability at all. It was my unsuitability to the job itself.

"I discovered I hated teaching basic skills just for the security of a paycheck. What I really wanted to do was write. That's what I'm doing now, but it took me five teaching jobs and a deep questioning of my father's views before I found what was right for me."

TODAY I will not blindly accept another's opinion without examining it in the light of my own experiences, abilities, and desires.

Our emotional and mental attitudes toward the disappointments in our lives can take many forms. Deep hurts or resentments can result in dissention, disease, or divorce. Loss of a loved one can be accompanied by mental illness and a loss of self-worth. Job dissatisfaction can result in fatigue, headaches, and increased irritability. Failing to meet our own or others'expectations can result in paralyzing guilt or a desire to punish ourselves.

Yet, the pain of dashed hopes needn't cripple us permanently if we take the time to uncover the cause of our despair. We can allow our discomfort to overwhelm us or we can allow it to work for us if we realize that our pain is often an indication of harmful attitudes that need to be discarded or changed for more wholesome and healthy attitudes.

Kahlil Gibran, author of **The Prophet,** describes the constructive use of pain in this way: "Much of your pain is self-chosen. It is the bitter potion by which the physician within you heals your sick self."

TODAY Let me realize I am responsible for much of the discomfort I feel. Since my attitudes have helped create the painful problem, I also have within me the healthy attitudes to solve it. I will work through my pain and heal self-limiting thoughts which prevent me from realizing my wholeness.

"Maybe you'll think I'm a crazy," said a friend, "but I'm grateful for the disappointments in my life. I even thank my Higher Power for every problem I experience."

"You see," she continued, "everytime I say, 'Thank You, God,' I am focusing on the solution, not the problem. I'm re-affirming my faith that there's a reason for whatever it is that's happening and that I'm supposed to learn something valuable from it.

"My saying, 'Thank You,' is also my way of admitting that I might have helped create the painful situation, and that I'm ready to receive the answer to my problem. Then I stop justifying my anger and bitterness and listen to my inner voice. It's amazing how many solutions unfold—and how many good reasons I can see for my problem—when I tune into that power within me!"

TODAY I will be grateful for my experiences. I know the answers to every problem are within me and within my grasp.

> "There is guidance for each of us, and by lowly listening we shall hear the right word. . . Place yourself in the middle of the stream of power and wisdom which flows into you as life, place yourself in the full center of that flood, then you are without effort impelled to truth, to right, and a perfect contentment."
>
> —Ralph Waldo Emerson

There are many gifts that can come from disappointments if we are open to them.

One such gift is the ability to help others. Having felt anger, guilt, and sorrow, we are better able to identify the same feelings in others. We can be more tolerant of others, and have compassion for those with similar hurts. And, if we overcome the pain of our own disappointments, we can share the attitudes and actions that helped us grow from those hurts.

Another gift is forgiveness. When we do not deny our pain—and make a concerted effort to work through our feelings of anger, rejection, and guilt—we gain a better perspective of ourselves and a better understanding of others. We become aware of our deepest desires and needs, our deepest insecurities and fears, our weaknesses and our strengths. When we can accept and understand our imperfect natures, we are more able to understand and forgive others their imperfections and growing pains.

TODAY I will use my disappointments as gifts to better understand myself as well as others. I will try to help others overcome their hurts by sharing my struggles and victories with them.

"He who knows himself, knows others."

—Charles C. Colton

How can disappointments be opportunities to grow? When we feel thwarted, frustrated or empty it is difficult—but not impossible—to see the positive side of our pain.

Most disappointments come from a sense of failure when our expectations of ourselves or others are not met. If we can work through our initial response of blaming others for our misfortunes and examine the source of frustration that lies within ourselves, we are taking the right steps toward turning our hurts and fears into growth-filled experiences.

Do we have unrealistic expectations of ourselves or others? Do we depend too much on other people's approval of us? Have we "sold ourselves short" by placing our entire self-worth on our jobs, paychecks, or possessions? Have we accepted negative feelings about ourselves, or do we see ourselves as capable human beings?

TODAY I will probe the sources of my self-esteem. I will seek my happiness within myself, not in other people, places, or things.

No matter what faces us—an unhappy relationship, a serious operation or illness, a feeling of uselessness or helplessness—it is vital to realize that there is a solution.

We must not expect that the solution to our problem will bring us immediate peace of mind. Focusing our energies and emotions on the answer—not the problem—will, however, alleviate much of the futility and frustration we feel.

A medical doctor, George S. Stevenson, wrote: "The solution may not give you everything you want. Sometimes, it may give you nothing but a chance to start all over again. But whatever little it gives you is much more than you give yourself by letting your emotions tear you apart."

TODAY I will focus my energies and emotions on the solution, not the problem. I will allow the solution to flow through me, with the help of my Higher Power, knowing there is a satisfactory answer to my difficulty.

Chapter 6

Aloneness and Quality Time

Before we can make any real progress, we must accept the essential fact of our "aloneness."

Accepting our aloneness means taking full responsibility for our actions, attitudes and neglects. We do not lean too heavily on others for our salvation or sense of purpose; we look inside ourselves for answers, alternatives, and right decisions. We regard others as mirrors in our journey toward self-discovery; we do not regard another as the Final Authority in our lives.

Recognizing our aloneness frees us from unhealthy dependence on any one person or thing for our sense of well-being. Our human relationships are put in their proper perspective. We no longer function from a position of "dire need." Rather, we function from a healthy desire to share our unique insights and experiences with others without any expectation of return.

TODAY I will accept my aloneness. I will not expect another, no matter how close to me, to be my savior. I will take full responsibility for my sense of meaning and purpose in life.

Many of us, in trying to run away from our essential aloneness, have abused alcohol, work, drugs, food, sex, money, and entertainment. In spite of our frantic activity, we have continued to feel "alone in a crowd," "alone in our dreams," and "lonely in our marriages."

These experiences should prove we cannot successfully avoid coming to terms with our aloneness. The sooner we accept responsibility for our lives, the sooner we will stop inflicting unnecessary pain on ourselves.

In accepting our aloneness, we accept that no one can protect us from ourselves—and that no one can live our lives for us. "Aloneness" simply means that we cannot depend on others for our joy or sorrow. We are the authors of our actions, attitudes, and experiences and not the "victims" of fate or circumstance.

TODAY I will not be afraid of my aloneness. I will accept total responsibility for my attitudes, actions, or neglects. I will not seek unnecessary pain by relying on what others say or do to make me happy.

Embracing our aloneness enables us to experience the fullness of life. Circumstances and relationships become gifts of enlightenment. Pain and joy become opportunities to learn more about ourselves and our interactions with life. Scientific discoveries become tools for understanding our inner selves as well as the laws which govern our natures and the universe.

Paradoxically, the more we accept our aloneness, the more we realize we are not alone. We begin to recognize our unity with all living things. Just as nature, for example, has its seasons and changes, so do we. Just as the sun warms us, so does a friend's smile. Just as the rain refreshes the earth, so our own tears refresh our spirits.

Far from isolating us from life, embracing our aloneness motivates us to invest and share ourselves with all living things. We begin to see our similarities with all Creation. We become one with the universe.

TODAY I will embrace my aloneness. I will invest myself in others and my environment. I will discover my similarities with all Creation.

We must give as much quality time to ourselves as we give to others. Otherwise, we will not have a healthy balance in our lives.

But what is "quality time" and what do we do with it? Quality time is time spent alone in the solitude of our own thoughts—without any outside distractions. Some of us go to a special place (the beach, a park, a room), others take solitary walks or drives, still others write in journals for a few minutes each day.

During our quiet moments, we review what we've done, thought, and said. We look at our motives. We try to detect any harmful attitudes or reactions that need improving. And we plan how best to correct our mistakes in the future. We also think about the things and people we are grateful for—and we thankfully note the gradual improvements in our relationships and circumstances as we continue to practice these principles in our daily lives.

TODAY I will spend quality time with myself.

> "Fortunate the man who has learned what to do in solitude and brought himself to see what companionship he may discover in it, what fortitude, what content."
>
> —William L. Sullivan

When we begin spending time alone, many of us may experience uncomfortable feelings. At first, we may be afraid of our thoughts. We feel that they are "not the right kind of thoughts" because they do not conform to what we've allowed ourselves to think or feel.

If we have conditioned ourselves not to feel angry, we may be frightened when bitter or hostile thoughts cross our minds. Or, if we have prided ourselves in being able to handle every situation, we may belittle ourselves when we experience a sense of helplessness in thinking about a job, home, or social situation.

The point of spending time in solitude is not to condemn ourselves but to get to know ourselves. In constructive solitude, we strive for awareness of our attitudes and reactions in terms of how they affect our daily lives. By observing their painful or peaceful results, we will then know what we wish to change or accept about ourselves.

TODAY I will use my time alone to observe myself. I will note the results of my attitudes and reactions in my life. I will keep those which bring me peace, and I will work on changing those which cause me pain.

Do we take time out of our busy schedules to enjoy what's most rewarding to us? Are we so burdened with troubles and duties we forget to take a few minutes to enjoy the uplifting aspects of life?

No matter how busy we are, all of us need to make time to engage in the things which make life worth living. In this way, we achieve a balanced view of ourselves and our world.

Writers of all cultures have seen the necessity of renewing our spirits with those things which bring us peace and joy. Robert Louis Stevenson enjoyed friendship: "A friend is the present you give yourself." Frances Perkins emphasized meditation: "It's only when we're relaxed that the thing way deep in all of us—call it the subconscious mind, the spirit, what you will—has a chance to well up and tell us how we should go." Lin Yutang stressed the importance of humor: "There is a purifying power in laughter. . ."

TODAY I will examine my ideas of joy and relaxation. I will take time in my busy day to do at least two things I enjoy.

Being good to ourselves involves setting priorities. In order to do this, we must spend some time thinking about what is most important to us.

What do we value? What are our goals? How best can we achieve them?

Making a list of our goals—whether they involve removing a shortcoming, establishing a new friendship, or spending more time with our children—and ranking them in their order of importance, is a valuable exercise in discovering what is most significant to us.

Once we are aware of our goals, we concentrate our attention and energies on the one or two most important ones. Then we ask ourselves, "How can we best attain these goals?" We must remember that if we do not limit our focus to one or two goals, we may set ourselves up for failure by taking on more than we can handle effectively.

TODAY I will work on one or two important goals. I will apply a valuable living principle in order to achieve this goal. I will not tackle any new project until I have made satisfactory progress on my current priorities.

There are many ways to be good to ourselves. Here are just a few:

At the beginning of each day, we can think about what we'd like to accomplish. This can be a routine household chore, a professional objective, or a living principle we'd like to work on.

As our day unfolds, we can engage in an enjoyable diversion or work on a pet project. Often, these activities clear our minds and free us to think more calmly about matters which trouble us.

In the evening, we may want to review the day's events, and our reactions to them, with a friend. Or, we may simply want to sit quietly and allow our thoughts to wander as they will. Keeping a journal at these times is a helpful tool for self-discovery. By recording our reactions and thoughts as they arise, we often get a better perspective on ourselves as well as our experiences.

TODAY I will be good to myself. I will find something I enjoy doing, and I will do it. I will also take time to get to know myself—either by sharing with a trusted friend or by writing my thoughts in a journal.

Weariness is a sign that our physical, mental, emotional, or spiritual energies are at a low point. To ignore this danger signal by driving ourselves even harder—often with the aid of stimulants, depressants or sheer self-will—is to invite disaster. When our inevitable collapse occurs, our old thought habits of fear, defeat, self-doubt, futility and helplessness can overwhelm us.

We can prevent becoming overwhelmed if we **stop** whatever we are doing at the first sign of fatigue.

"H.A.L.T.!" urged a woman at a meeting, "whenever you're too HUNGRY, ANGRY, LONELY, or TIRED. Stop and fill whatever need you've overlooked in over-extending yourself. If you're hungry, eat. If you're angry, deal with your anger and its cause. If you're lonely, take time to talk with God or a friend. And if you're tired, rest. If you H.A.L.T. until your needs are filled, fatigue can be a friend."

TODAY I will H.A.L.T. when I feel exhausted. I will discover what physical, mental, emotional, or spiritual need is lacking, and I will fill it.

Chapter 7

Blame and Criticism

We must be careful not to take what others say too personally. None of us can be totally objective when we listen to or share our thoughts and feelings. Our communication, and that of others, is limited by our separate experiences, hurts, frustrations, values and hopes.

Once we realize that living is a very subjective experience, we need not be "victims" of others' opinions of us. Criticism and praise alike can be taken in equal stride. Our task is to carefully weigh the accuracy of another's self-projection to see whether or not it is valid for us. Since each person can only respond to us the way he or she regards him or herself, we must delve beneath surface comments to understand what that person is going through, or has gone through, before we can apply his or her opinions to our own lives.

TODAY I will be careful not to take what another says to me, or about me, too personally. I know each person, including myself, is limited by subjective experiences, feelings and insights.

> "One must judge men not by their opinions, but by what their opinions have made of them."
>
> —Georg Lichtenberg

> "As a solid rock is not shaken by the wind, so the wise man does not waver before blame or praise."
>
> —Buddhist Proverb

How often we hear ourselves saying, "If he would only do this. . ." or "If she would only change that, **then** I would be happier and everything would be all right!"

How often we delude ourselves into thinking that all our problems would disappear if only someone **else** would "shape up" or change.

And yet, if we are really honest with ourselves, we can remember times when he **did** what we wanted, and she **did** change. But we were **still** unhappy and dissatisfied.

These experiences, if we choose to remember them, should convince us that true happiness and serenity come from changing ourselves, and **not** in forcing changes in others.

TODAY I am aware that the only cause of my happiness or sorrow is me. No other person or circumstance can hurt me unless I allow it. I will take each event that happens today as an opportunity to discover something new about myself, and I will grow from it.

> "My improvement does not depend on forcing changes in someone else."

Blaming someone or something else for the unhappiness in our lives rarely solves anything. Constant complaining, whether silent or spoken, distances us from the real cause of our misery and prevents us from growing up.

Blaming or complaining attitudes such as, "He made me do it!" "It's all her fault." "I had no other choice," "Everyone else is doing it," "No one understands me," "I don't have any friends," "He deserved what he got," "I'll show **her**," and "I won't apologize until **he** does," are all examples of the childish reactions we often carry into our adult lives.

Not until we are willing to take responsibility for our **own** attitudes, actions, and neglects—without blaming others for them—will we find the inner peace and harmony we are all searching for.

TODAY I will stop and listen to my silent and spoken thoughts. Do I hear myself complaining or blaming a lot? If so, I will turn my attention to the real source of unhappiness: my dissatisfaction with me.

Taking responsibility for our own attitudes, actions, and neglects is far more difficult than managing and directing other people's lives.

Giving advice to another, for example, is much easier that practicing what we preach. If we would apply our advice to our **own** lives, we would have less time to criticize, correct, or interfere in someone else's difficulties. Moreover, we would be amazed at how many alternatives we have within our own grasp that could solve, or at least alleviate, the problems in our lives.

TODAY Let me realize I am far more positive and productive when I concentrate my efforts and thoughts on changing myself and my own actions. Give me the courage to act on my own internal wisdom.

> "There's only one corner of the universe you can be certain of improving, and that's your own self. So you have to begin there, not outside, not on other people. That comes afterward, when you've worked on your own corner."
>
> —Aldous Huxley

When we no longer find satisfaction in our most cherished beliefs and begin to doubt our own habitual reactions and opinions, we are ready to start life anew.

Many of us, however, regard this turning point in our lives as a sign of "weakness." Disgusted with ourselves, we often disguise our emptiness by blaming our family members, our "rotten" childhood, our jobs, "shifty-eyed" politicians, our ill-health,or our "miserable" friendships. But the real lack is within ourselves; it is not in any other person, outside circumstance, or institution.

Once we admit this lack, and take the necessary steps to fill it with new ideas and attitudes, we come to see that our greatest "weaknesses" are the very avenues to greater growth, happiness, and serenity.

TODAY If I am feeling empty or frustrated, I will not blame anyone but myself. I will realize that my unsettling emotions are indications of my need for change, new insights, and growth.

> "One must never lose time in vainly regretting the past or in complaining against the changes which cause us discomfort, for change is the essence of life."
>
> —Anatole France

Have we a distrust of others? Are we afraid of intimacy? Are we uncomfortable when we communicate our deepest thoughts and desires? Do we fear rejection or possession by others?

All of our fears come from a lack of trust in ourselves, not in others. We can only fear in others what we have not conquered in ourselves. If we fear others will control us, then we do not feel in control of our own lives. If we fear rejection, we may have rejected something we cherish in ourselves. If we are suspicious of others' motives and actions, very likely we doubt our own. And if we disdain the hypocrisy in others, perhaps we also condemn ourselves when we do not live up to our highest ideals and expectations.

Thomas a'Kempis, fifteenth century German scholar and monk, wrote: "He that is in perfect peace suspects no one, but he that is discontented and disturbed is tossed about with various suspicions; he is neither quiet himself nor does he allow others to be quiet."

TODAY Let me remind myself that it is **not** distrust of others I must fear, but distrust of myself.

> "As soon as you trust yourself you will know how to live."
>
> —Goethe

Excessive criticism, resentment, and self-righteousness are often symptoms of our refusal to grow and change. Until we recognize these symptoms as merely the outward effects of self-imposed stagnation, we cannot change the unhappy circumstances in our lives.

Once we admit that our lives are not all they could be, that we do not have all the answers, and that we really do desire to change, we can begin making progress.

To make any real progress, however, we will have to be open to many new ideas and opinions we would normally fight and resist. Many of the things we hear at meetings, for example, will jar the security of our old notions and beliefs. If we are not receptive to these new ideas, we may shut out the very guidance and perspectives that can help us find the inner peace and fulfillment we are looking for.

TODAY I will listen and share with an open mind. I will not resist a new idea by becoming defensive or self-righteous. I will try to apply what I hear to my own life.

Am I bored? Highly critical? Fearful or anxious? If the answer to any of these questions is "yes," I may be suffering the effects of procrastination.

If I am plagued by boredom, I may not be seeking or initiating constructive changes in my life. By refusing to ask questions or seek answers to questions I already have, for instance, I perpetuate my sense of failure and emptiness.

If I am highly critical of others, it is very likely I am a "non-doer." People who are busy **doing** their heart's desires have little time to complain about the actions or attitudes of others.

If I am anxious or fearful about the future, I may be postponing until tomorrow what I could be doing today. Merely hoping or wishing my life will get better, while avoiding or worrying about an unpleasant task or problem, is self-defeating at best. If I want to live today fully, I must do something constructive with it.

TODAY I will tackle at least two things I dread doing. I will not waste my time and energy by wallowing in boredom, worry, criticism, or fear. I will do what needs to be done even if it requires effort, risk and change.

The more we practice this positive living philosophy, one day at a time, the more we see that the faults we criticize in others are the same shortcomings we have within ourselves. These faults are those which we either haven't forgiven ourselves for, or haven't had the courage to face squarely.

If we are to be true and loving toward ourselves, we will want to change our hostile and bitter attitudes toward ourselves and others by accepting that neither we—nor our friends, loved ones, or acquaintances—have attained the perfection we all desire. We will want to learn to forgive ourselves and each other for our growing pains and internal struggles. These pains and struggles will someday lead us to the perfection and peace of mind for which we are all searching.

TODAY I will look upon myself and others with dignity. I will see myself and those I meet as equals in spirit, for we are all searching children of a loving Creator.

> "God has put something noble and good into every heart which His hand created."
>
> —Mark Twain

Chapter 8

Attitudes and Limitations

The wisdom of all ages and cultures emphasizes the tremendous power our thoughts have over our character and circumstances.

The proverbs of the Judeo-Christian Bible say: "As a man thinketh in his heart, so is he." "Keep thy heart with all diligence, for out of it are the issues of life." The Upanishads of Hinduism state: "Let a man purify his thoughts. . . Man becomes that of which he thinks." The Dhamapada of Buddhism reiterate: "All that we are is the result of what we have thought. The mind is everything. What we think, we become."

By the thoughts we choose to cultivate and encourage, we author our experiences and character. The failures and successes in our lives are merely the effects of our destructive or constructive thoughts. Harmonious and loving attitudes bring peace and joy; inharmonious and fear-filled attitudes result in pain and conflict.

TODAY I will respect the power of my mind. I will rise above doubt, fear, and despair by uplifting my thoughts and by acting upon them.

To a large extent, the way we think determines who we are and what happens to us.

We cannot harbor poisonous thoughts without their effects visibly showing in our lives. If we dwell on our inadequacy and ineffectiveness, for example, circumstances will prove us correct because we will invite self-defeating events to us.

On the other hand, replacing destructive thoughts with hope-filled, optimistic ones brings peaceful and confidence-producing circumstances to us. We will radiate competence and joy.

We would be wise, therefore, to take the advice of twentieth century author Orison Swett Marden: "Stoutly determine not to harbor anything in the mind which you do not wish to become real in your life. Shun poisoned thoughts, ideas which depress and make you unhappy, as instinctively as you avoid physical danger of any kind—replace all these with cheerful, hopeful, optimistic thoughts."

TODAY I will make it a habit to continually replace pessimistic thoughts with optimistic ones. I will dwell on what is uplifting so that I may increase my courage and confidence as well as better my circumstances.

Each of us, to some extent, is limited by our childhood experiences. Much of what we currently think and feel—consciously or unconsciously—is the result of our parents' attitudes, actions, and reactions toward life. Unless we become aware of, and **admit** that we share many of our parents' erroneous attitudes and actions, we are destined to repeat them.

A fellow illustrated this point when he said: "I hated my parents' constant criticism of me. I swore I'd never be like them. Yet, when I had children of my own, I found myself pointing out their faults. I was also silently critical of my co-workers.

"My parents were also afraid of what the neighbors would think. Now, guess who doesn't do anything different for fear of others' opinions? Me!"

It is not enough to "will away" our dissatisfactions. Fighting our past only brings it upon us. Until we learn to surrender to our imperfections and admit our limitations, we cannot receive new insight and understanding to correct our mistakes.

TODAY I will not fight my own or others' limitations. I will admit my imperfections so that I can grow from them.

Mere attendance at meetings or church does not solve our problems overnight. We may be accepted by our peers and inspired by much of what we hear, but our progress will be limited if we do not **apply** what we learn to our daily lives.

It is all too easy to fall back into destructive ways of thinking and reacting if we do not keep daily watch on our thoughts and attitudes. We must continually **replace** our negative reactions with constructive ones.

When we begin dreading the future, we must remind ourselves we can only live **one day at a time.** When we hear ourselves blaming others, we must remember we can only change **ourselves.** When we feel the need to justify our shortcomings and resentments, we must practice self-honesty and forgiveness. It is only by the daily practice of uplifting thoughts that we can conquer our old, debilitating habits and beliefs.

TODAY I will redouble my efforts to **replace** negative attitudes with positive ones.

> "You yourself must make the effort. The Buddhas are only teachers."
>
> —Buddhist Proverb

What we consider our greatest strengths can also be our greatest weaknesses.

Excessive pride in "being able to handle everything," for example, may result in our taking on other people's responsibilities. In "taking over," we often lessen another's desire to meet his or her own obligations.

A boastful "I'll do it myself!" attitude can also mask a desperate feeling of inadequacy. Having a constant drive to "prove" our worth to others, we may trample on, or ignore, the needs of those around us who are just as eager to exhibit their competency and worth.

What are some other examples of virtues becoming vices?

Determination, to excess, becomes obstinacy and stubbornness. Honesty, when misdirected, is synonymous with gossip and slander. Sympathy and concern, overdone, can cripple and smother.

TODAY I will make a list of ten of my strengths and weaknesses. How has acting on each of these virtues and vices created joy or sorrow in my life? I will be aware that my strengths can be my worst enemies if I abuse them.

All of us have unique talents and gifts. No obstacle, be it physical, mental, or emotional, has the power to destroy our innate creative energies.

In order to tap our inner resources, we must first be willing to explore our interests and abilities. Then we need to make persistent efforts to acquire the necessary skills and knowledge which will help us achieve our highest potentials.

Helen Keller's life story is an excellent example of this kind of courage and persistence. With the help of her teacher, Anne Sullivan, Helen learned to speak and read. Because Helen did not allow her blindness and deafness to destroy her innate gifts, she inspired millions to challenge their own physical, mental, and emotional handicaps and limitations.

TODAY I will not allow my limitations to overwhelm me. I will see them as challenges that I and others can benefit from. I will acquire any new skills or information I need to make my limitations work **for** me, not against me.

> "I thank God for my handicaps, for, through them, I have found myself, my work, and my God."
>
> —Helen Keller

"I have learned," admitted a fellow, "that intelligence is **not** the same as wisdom. It is only when I try to apply, and practice, the knowledge I do have that I discover whether my opinions and beliefs are helpful or not.

"Most of my life I have flaunted my knowledge without really living it, so I never knew if what I was saying was true. Mostly, I used my 'superior intellect' to win arguments and hide my fear of inferiority. Eventually, my friends couldn't stand me and avoided my company. When I was left alone, I found how empty my intellectualizations were without an active adversary.

"Now I know that the true test of whether my intelligence is really wisdom is to see if **acting** upon it **improves** my life. If my 'intelligent actions' don't give me any peaceful or practical results, then I'd better become 'stupid' enough to find out what does!"

TODAY I will place more value on common sense and wisdom than on unapplied intelligence and knowledge.

> "Very often the ones with the greatest 'book learning' have a remarkably poor understanding of life in general. Wisdom comes from doing battle with life's problems, not from simply reading about them."
>
> —Author Unknown

James Allen, in his book **As A Man Thinketh,** states that our outer circumstances are a direct result of our inner attitudes.

At first, this may be a difficult idea to swallow. It is so much easier to believe we are the "victims" of forces beyond our control. Until we grow beyond our childish notion that we are limited by our past, our environment, our poverty—or whatever else we are claiming is the cause of our unhappiness—we can make little progress in bettering ourselves or improving our situation.

We choose, consciously or unconsciously, the circumstances in our lives. Our very attitudes and reactions to ourselves, others, and our world create our experiences. Abraham Lincoln reaffirmed this idea when he said, "Most folks are about as happy as they make up their minds to be." The Koran expresses the cause of our misery this way: "And whatsoever suffering ye suffer, it is what your hands have wrought."

These ideas, as old as history itself, ask us to be accountable for, and to, ourselves. We need to become increasingly aware of our deepest attitudes and motives if we wish to rise above our circumstances.

TODAY I am not the victim of other people's attitudes, actions and neglects. I am free to choose my thoughts and actions. By choosing wisely, I can transform any of the unwanted conditions in my life.

> "The divinity that shapes our ends is in ourselves. . .All that a man achieves or fails to achieve is the direct result of his own thoughts."
>
> —James Allen

"My greatest limitations," a member said, "are in my mind. Until I came to this group, I wasn't even aware that many of the negative circumstances in my life were the direct result of my distorted attitudes.

"I brought myself a lot of unnecessary misery by thinking it was my responsibility to manage and direct other people's lives. I believed it was solely up to me to make everyone else happy and secure. So I continually placed everyone else's needs first until I didn't know who I was or what I needed for my own happiness and comfort. It's exhausting and insane to try to second-guess everyone. Not only that, it doesn't give me or anyone else credit for being able to think, feel, or act for himself."

TODAY I will not manage or direct other people's lives, nor will I expect any other human being to fill my inner emptiness. I have the dignity, resources, and responsibility to fulfill my own life just as others have theirs. I will find my own sources of comfort, joy, and peace no matter what others do with their lives and free choices.

Chapter 9
Courage and Patience

"One of the hardest lessons for me to learn is patience," admitted a fellow. "I've been in a race all my life. I suppose I could compare myself to the hare in the fable of 'The Tortoise and the Hare.' I jump into things, rush at them, and never seem to cross the finish line. I get side-tracked by other things that seem to need immediate attention. I never have a sense of peace. Everything has to be done by yesterday.

"I was even in a hurry in my marriage—which is one reason I'm divorced now. I wanted my wife to race with me. I wanted her to be perfect overnight. I nagged at her constantly. I was too impatient to let her grow at her own speed. Because I couldn't slow down, I couldn't allow her to be at peace either.

"I thought I was doing all the changing and growing, when, in reality, all I was doing was bombarding my problems and projects with a lot of momentum and very little common sense."

TODAY I will slow down. I only increase my difficulties when I try to solve them in a hurry.

"Slow motion gets you there faster."

—Hoagy Carmichael

Courage is not grim determination, boastful arrogance, or uncontrolled aggression. True courage comes from quiet conviction which shows itself in self-control, calm assurance, and patient persistence.

It takes courage, for example, to resist lashing back at others who hurt or offend us. It takes courage to endure the consequences of our attitudes, actions, and neglects without bragging or complaining. It takes courage to believe no situation or person is hopeless. It takes courage to remain optimistic about life when nothing seems to turn out right. It takes courage to maintain our enthusiasm and effort despite delays and setbacks. It takes courage to do the things we know are right in spite of our fears of rejection or inadequacy. And it takes courage to refrain from taking over a loved one's responsibilities when he or she is failing to meet them.

TODAY I will face life with courage. I will respond calmly and confidently to life's challenges. I will place my faith and trust in God and the principles I am learning in this philosophy of living.

persistence = courage
my persistence in
eating properly is my
courage today.

If we think about the principles and opinions expressed in each of these meditations and apply these concepts to our lives **one day at a time,** we will experience a peace of mind and joy we never thought possible.

By the daily practice of this living philosophy, we can take control of our lives, have more harmonious relationships, improve our present circumstances, increase our faith and hope in the future, and attain greater health than we have ever known before.

What progress we make, however, will only be the result of the efforts we put into these principles. Ultimate victory over ourselves and our difficult circumstances will not be achieved overnight. Peace of mind, a sense of renewed purpose, joy, improved health, loving relationships, deeper understanding and faith, whatever it is that we are searching for, can only be attained by the constant opening and disciplining of our minds and hearts.

TODAY I will accept the challenge of living an abundant, peace-filled, and purpose-filled life. I will make whatever efforts are necessary to achieve my deepest dreams and desires.

Continuous effort—not strength or intelligence—is the key to unlocking and using our potential.

Most of us, however, have convinced ourselves we do not have "what it takes" to achieve our life's dream. We complain about our lack of this and that (education, opportunities, money, health, youth) or we stubbornly cling to our comfortable (if joyless) securities as the reasons for not pursuing greater satisfaction and fulfillment.

Trapped by our doubts and fears, we blame the "social system" or others for our own lack of effort and initiative.

Those of us, however, who have challenged our fears and taken the necessary risks to find our life's work, have never regretted it. Our few defeats have made our numerous successes well worth our persistent efforts.

TODAY I will work toward my dream no matter what obstacles face me. In persevering I will attain my goal.

"Our doubts are traitors,
And make us lose the good we oft might win
By fearing to attempt."

—William Shakespeare

There are times when the "poor me" mood strikes us all. We complain that things are not better. We bemoan our sorry lot in life. We condemn ourselves and others for not meeting our expectations.

What can we do when these destructive emotions engulf us? First, we can realize that our "self-pity" is often the result of comparing ourselves with others or to some unrealistic standard of perfection that we think we "should" have reached and have not.

What we need to do at times like these is take a fresh look at ourselves and our circumstances. We must evaluate ourselves in relation **to ourselves,** and avoid comparisons with others.

When we view our progress honestly and clearly, in comparison to our own past performances and our own present conditions, we get a better perspective on the strides we have made. Seeing our growth, we can patiently bear our current frustrations because we have overcome our previous struggles and disillusionments.

TODAY I am in competition with no one. I shall seek to better myself by growing beyond where I am. I will be patient with myself and take small steps. I will not expect perfection overnight.

Let us review what others have written about courage and patience:

"Courage is fear that has said its prayers." —Anonymous

"All things come to him who waits—provided he knows what he is waiting for." —Woodrow Wilson

"Courage is more than standing for a firm conviction. It includes the risk of **questioning** that conviction." —Julian Weber Gordon

"How poor are they who have not patience! What wound did ever heal but by degrees?" —William Shakespeare

"It takes time to succeed because success is merely the natural reward for taking time to do anything well." —Joseph Ross

"Courage is what it takes to stand up and speak; courage is also what it takes to sit down and listen." —Anonymous

TODAY I will ask myself, "In what areas do I need more courage and patience?" I will pick one thought that most applies to me, and I will work on improving that part of my character.

"The best way I know to tell the difference between patience and procrastination," a friend said, "is to look at my motives for my actions or inactions.

"If I delay doing something out of fear and self-doubt, then I'm procrastinating. I'm letting irrational emotions dictate my behavior.

"If, on the other hand, I delay doing something because I'm waiting for the outcome of something I've already worked on, that's patience. Patience is calm and rational. It is the result of confidence and hard work. I'm not 'putting off' anything because I've already **done** everything in my power to achieve my goal. Instead, I'm putting the results of my efforts in God's hands with the assurance I've done my best and can do no more."

TODAY Am I being patient, or am I procrastinating? I will not let fear or self-doubt govern my behavior. I will stop procrastinating on the things I need to do, and then I will patiently place the results of my efforts in God's hands.

> "Procrastination usually results in sorrowful regret. Today's duties put off until tomorrow give us a double burden to bear; the best way is to do them in their proper time."
>
> —Ida Scott Taylor

This powerful living philosophy—as helpful, healing, and hopeful as it is—can do little for those who do not wish to make any consistent effort to change or improve themselves. Those who come to meetings for someone or something other than themselves—or those who attend seeking momentary escape from the pressing problems in their lives—will receive exactly what they've come for: a temporary solution and a fleeting feeling of well-being.

Those, however, who have a sincere desire to change, those who are not expecting "easy" or "comfortable" solutions, those who are willing to make the minute-by-minute effort to apply these principles to every area of their lives, will reap the rich rewards of increased peace of mind, happiness, and inner fulfillment.

TODAY I will not expect my search for peace of mind to come in the form of "easy" answers. I will do whatever I need to do and face whatever I need to face to gain the improvements I want in my life.

> "It is no easy thing for a principle to become a man's own unless each day he maintain it and work it out in his life."
>
> —Epictetus

Chapter 10

Depression and Despair

All of us get "the blues" now and then. Some of our depressions can last a few hours; others can last a few weeks or months. What are some of the causes of these low periods, and what can we do about them?

"I believe I get depressed when I'm stuck somewhere in my life," a woman explained. "I grow to a certain point, and then I stop growing. Something needs changing, but I'm not sure what.

"At other times, my depressions are caused by excessive worry. I'm thinking way into the future or dwelling remorsefully on the past. Sometimes I'm low because I'm bored. I'm not using my fullest potential because I don't know what I can do and am too lazy to find out. I also get the blues when I'm lonely and am too proud to call a friend or feel too inadequate to meet people.

"I find talking my feelings out with a close friend a great help in discovering the cause of my depressions. Once I understand what's keeping me stuck, I can change and begin growing again. I can either go around the obstacle or remove it altogether."

TODAY I realize that the first step in overcoming the blues is to become aware of what is causing them. I shall seek the counsel of others to help me get "unstuck."

Do we go about our daily work dutifully but joylessly? Have we settled for less in our jobs, homes, or relationships than we want? Have we substituted financial security or physical comfort for the freedom to pursue our heart's desires?

Very few of us give ourselves the opportunities to explore our real interests and potentials. We "lock" ourselves into rigid ways of regarding the world and our options. We often settle for less than our highest aspirations because we have conditioned ourselves into thinking life is joyless endurance or survival at best.

In order to change the empty circumstances in our lives we need to change our limited thinking patterns. Instead of looking at life as a prison, we can view it as a smorgasbord of opportunities that are well within our reach. By exploring and sampling the choices before us we can discover which choices bring us inner satisfaction and increase our sense of purpose.

TODAY I will remind myself of what Roman philosopher Seneca said hundreds of years ago: "The great blessings of mankind are within us, and within our reach. . ."

"Every time I over-extend myself, I fall into my old ways of thinking and reacting," states a long-time member. "When I'm tired, I lose all perspective and control. I over-react to the littlest things. I'm suspicious and paranoid. I get frustrated and discouraged easily. And I think defeatist thoughts like, 'What's the use?' 'Who cares?' 'I don't have anything to offer anyone!' 'Why don't I just give up?' 'I wish everyone would stop bothering me.' Fatigue sure brings out the worst in me. That's why I make every effort to balance my work time with rest and relaxation. It's too easy to drive myself to the point of despair and desperation when I don't pace myself."

TODAY I realize that much of my despair and discouragement comes from taking on too much. I will learn to pace myself so that I do not fall into my old negative thinking patterns.

> "People have not learned the blessed art of restful living and laboring. Everything they do is a burden to them. At work, at play, they are living tired, strained lives. God did not mean for people to live in this manner. One of this generation's greatest needs is rest."
>
> —Rev. James H. Taylor

Our greatest limitations reside in our destructive thinking patterns. Most of us, however, do not realize we have self-defeating beliefs or values until we lose something we treasure (a loved one, our health, a job, etc.), or no longer find fulfillment in the people and things we once cherished.

When we seek outside help in our despair—whether it's from a professional, a support group, a close friend, or God—we have the opportunity to uncover many of the causes of our unhappiness.

We may discover, for instance, that our childish notion of God (as a jolly Santa Claus, a demanding parent, a punishing policeman, etc.) is no longer sufficient for our adult needs. We may find, too, that our childish desires for wealth, possessions, approval, and fame are no longer as important as our inner desires for peace of mind, wisdom, and truth.

TODAY I will examine any harmful ideas or habits which are keeping me in bondage. I will seek the help of others I admire and respect to enable me to uncover the old attitudes and views I no longer need.

"Concentrating on what I lack keeps me in despair," confesses someone. "I can't make decisions. I fret about the future. I fear the present, and I feel totally inadequate to deal with anyone or anything effectively. What can I do?"

If we continually dwell on the things we don't have, we block the flow of creative ideas within us as well as those which could flow to us. Focusing on lack produces lack; hopelessness and depression result from this kind of "empty" thinking.

We can prevent despair by replacing "lack" thoughts with "abundance" thoughts whenever a limiting idea crosses our minds. We can visualize our competence, success, and achievement no matter what apparent obstacle faces us.

TODAY I will not let adverse circumstances defeat me. I will picture myself attaining my goal. I will thank God for supplying me with what I personally need to achieve my worthwhile goal.

> "Every worthwhile accomplishment, big or
> little, has its stages of drudgery and
> triumph; a beginning, a struggle, and
> a victory."

—Anonymous

What am I doing with what I've got? Instead of despairing over my lack of abilities in certain areas, am I doing the best with the talents I've been given?

All of us have unique gifts and abilities. Some of us work well with our hands; others are gifted at working with abstract ideas. Whatever our abilities, we would do well to concentrate on bringing those we **can do** to fruition rather than focus on our limitations.

Greek philosopher Epictetus put it this way: "He is a wise man who does not grieve for the things which he has not, but rejoices for those which he has." German poet and dramatist Goethe said: "The man who is born with a talent which he is meant to use finds his greatest happiness in using it."

TODAY Let me not concentrate on my handicaps as much as on my abilities. I know I have been given all I need to make my life a success.

> "Rebellion against your handicaps gets you nowhere. Self-pity gets you nowhere. One must have the adventurous daring to accept oneself as a bundle of possibilities and undertake the most interesting game in the world—making the most of one's best."
>
> —Harry Emerson Fosdick

How many of us have given up on or forgotten our childhood dreams? How many of us have scoffed at our daydreams or fantasies? Rather than condemn ourselves for our rich imaginations, we would be wise to pay close attention to them. Our dreams may be the seeds of realities we are meant to live!

Mencius, an early disciple of Confucius, wrote: "The great man is he who does not lose his child's heart." Jules Verne, a nineteenth century French novelist, asserted: "Anything one man can imagine, other men can make real." American naturalist and writer Henry David Thoreau declared: "If you have built castles in the air your work need not be lost; that is where they should be. Now put foundations under them."

TODAY I affirm that my dreams are God-given. I will consciously examine my dreams and decide how best to pursue them. I will not stop my efforts until I have made my dream a reality.

> "Far away there in the sunshine are my highest aspirations. I may not reach them, but I can look up and see their beauty, believe in them, and try to follow where they lead."
>
> —Louisa May Alcott

We need to make plans and carry them out, whether it's a schedule of things needing to be done to insure our physical survival and comfort or a mentally fulfilling goal we want to reach in the future. If we do not have a satisfying goal, if we are not working on at least one important priority, our lives can become meaningless.

We must also realize that we may never experience a total sense of accomplishment or self-satisfaction once we achieve our desired goal or goals. This is as it should be, for our journey toward perfection is just that: a journey. The joy comes more in the journey than in our "arrival." It is our ever-continuing progress that matters, not our perfection. We must constantly renew ourselves and grow beyond where we are.

TODAY Let me see life as an exciting journey, not a destination. If I achieve my goal today, I will use that accomplishment as a stepping stone to explore my deeper inner resources, abilities, interests, and opportunities.

> "Bad will be the day for every man when he becomes absolutely contented with the life he is living, when there is not forever beating at the doors of his soul some great desire to do something larger."
>
> —Phillips Brooks

Let us examine our ideas of recreation and pleasure. What activities do we enjoy that refresh our sagging spirits? Do we give ourselves a little time, each day, to be good to ourselves? Or do we continually immerse ourselves in dead-end thoughts of our powerlessness and frustration?

All of us have some particular interest or hobby that gives us a sense of peace and satisfaction. It may be something which produces tangible results (like picture-taking, gardening, sewing, remodeling, writing, or jogging), or it may be something which produces no immediate results (like meditating, reading, observing nature, praying, going to a movie, or helping a friend with a problem).

Whatever our individual interest is, we would be wise to balance our frustration with joy by taking time out to pursue what is uniquely meaningful and relaxing to us.

TODAY I will take at least thirty minutes to be good to myself. I will engage in an activity personally fulfilling so that I may refresh my spirit and clear my mind.

> "He who sees how action may be rest and rest action—he is wisest among his kind; he has the truth. He does well acting or resting."
>
> —Hindu Saying

"Depressions are transition times for me," an older fellow stated. "I look at my lows as a preparation period, an inner time of growth and change even though I'm not consciously aware of what's going on inside me. But I didn't always think this way.

"I used to get terrified when I got into one of those low periods. Every time I did, I questioned everything I ever believed in. I doubted myself and my abilities, my opinions and values, my friends and my boss. Nothing escaped my painful questioning. I thought for sure I was going insane. The pain was so unbearable I wanted to drink, work harder, have more sex, **anything,** to distract me from my anguish.

"Now, when I get low, I take it more in stride. I think of my depression as part of a natural cycle. Just as nature has its fall, winter, and spring; I, too, have a period of shedding old growth for new growth. I just endure my grey days knowing the sun will shine again—just as the trees will bloom after winter. As part of the natural world around me, I, too, have my seasons of joy and sorrow."

TODAY I will remember that my lows are as natural as my highs. I will not become overwhelmed and exaggerate the significance of my depressions. I will endure patiently, knowing that whatever faces me will pass in time.

Chapter 11

Listening and Sharing

The greatest gift we can give another person is the gift of ourselves. When we can share our deepest convictions and failures, our ideals and disillusionments, our hopes and frustrations, our dreams and despairs, our answers and our questions—then we are loving our neighbors as ourselves as well as "loving our enemies."

A friend put it this way: "If I share the whole of me with you, I share the good as well as the bad. I don't hide anything of myself from you, not in a deep friendship, or a deep marriage for that matter. By sharing some things I hate about myself, I'm loving my inside enemy. I'm telling you I'm still human and have a lot of growing to do. I'd love to tell you about all my good points; it would make me feel a lot better, but it wouldn't be sharing **all** of me with you."

TODAY I will concentrate on sharing my insides and outsides with another. I will listen to myself as I talk. I will not be satisfied if I sit on my laurels or wallow in my woes. I will improve myself by becoming aware of how I communicate to others.

American psychologist Abraham Maslow believed human beings communicate on one of five levels at any given time.

The first level, and the most shallow, is the cliche level: "Hi, how are you?" "Fine." At this level, we ask a question or respond to one out of politeness, but we really do not want to receive or give a truthful answer.

The second level of communication involves two people speaking of a third party or thing. Quite often, this kind of sharing deteriorates into gossip. In talking about others we often avoid depth or any real sharing of our inner selves.

On the third level, two people talk about a subject such as politics, religion, education, and so forth. At this level, we show a little more of our inside selves, our ideals, but we do not reveal the reality we actually live.

The fourth, increasingly deeper, level of communication comes when we share our hopes and hurts, joys and mistakes, dreams and fears. It is at this level that we share who we really are; it is our gift of love, the gift of ourselves.

The fifth level is the listening and receiving level. We receive love from others when we listen to their deepest longings and disappointments.

TODAY I will give from my heart and receive another into my heart. I will meet a new friend in myself and in another.

To **assume** what other people are thinking or feeling, without asking them, is to invite misunderstanding. Just as disastrous is to **assume** other people know what we want or need without our telling them. Many potentially good friendships and marriages perish because of our false assumptions and our lack of honest communication.

Do we assume others can't live without us or wouldn't know what to think or feel unless we told them? Do we take for granted that "silence means assent"? Do we assume others don't have time for us, or don't care about us, if they don't call or go out of their way to talk to us? Do we think others can read our minds without our ever opening our mouths?

Since we can only assume the same limited or distorted thoughts of others that we have of ourselves, we each need to take the initiative to ask probing questions and give honest responses in our relationships.

TODAY I will not make the mistake of projecting my feelings onto others. I will initiate honest and open communication.

"I've found that many of my painful experiences with others are the result of past memories," stated a friend. "Often I'm not reacting so much to what is going on between me and another person right at the time; I'm responding to some previous wound or hurt from my past that hasn't quite healed. Let me give you an example of what I mean.

"Just the other day, a friend of mine said she needed some time to herself and didn't want to see me for a week. Well, rather than accept her statement, I was hurt. I immediately thought of a past friendship I had helped destroy by being too possessive and demanding. I thought I was making the same mistake again and that my present girl friend was trying to get rid of me, too. I felt so defeated I couldn't respond. I just sat there stunned and tried not to cry.

"My friend was uncomfortable with my change in attitude, but since I wasn't able to communicate what I was feeling, she left feeling at loose ends, too."

"Thank goodness I had enough sense to call her and share my unsettling feelings a day or two after that experience. I found my friend wasn't rejecting me at all. She really did need some time to herself."

TODAY I will not allow past, painful memories to cripple my current relationships. When I am hurt or confused, I will talk out my feelings and reactions before I make harsh criticisms or assume another's motives.

Do we say "Yes" or "Yes, BUT. . . ." to people in our lives?

Saying "Yes, but. . ." can be a way to avoid facing ourselves and the choices before us. "Yes, but. . ." means "I refuse to change," "You don't understand the situation," or "My case is so much more difficult, I can't possibly do what you suggest." All too often we justify our self-destructive behavior and negative thinking patterns with our self-righteous "Yes, but. . ." attitude.

Instead of concentrating on why we **can't** do a thing, we would be wise to change our "Yes, but. . ." attitude to a more positive one. Saying "Yes" to another's criticism can often open our minds to new ways of thinking and acting. Saying "Yes " means "I really do want to change my life for the better," "You may be right," and "I'll consider your suggestion."

TODAY If I find myself responding with too many "Yes, but's" I will practice saying "Yes." I will be open to new ways of thinking and acting. I will look for my **similarities** with others, not my differences.

"From the cowardice that shrinks
from new truth,
From the laziness that is content
with half-truths,
From the arrogance that thinks it
knows all truth,
Oh, God of Truth, deliver us."

—Ancient Hebrew Prayer

As this prayer suggests, changing our attitudes and reactions to what others say and do is not easy. Our pride, fear, and laziness often prevent us from receiving new insights so necessary to our growth.

For many of us, justifying our old ideas, even when those ideas have resulted in continual heartache, has become a way of life.

If we wish to replace this self-destructive habit with a constructive one, we need to be more tolerant of other people's views. We need to accept the fact that we do not have all the answers. We need to realize that each person we meet has a part of a larger truth. We must also remember that receiving new insight does not come without some pain or discomfort.

TODAY I will listen with respect. I will make a conscious and courageous effort to apply what I hear to my own life. I will expand my knowledge of truth and wisdom.

Most of us make trouble for ourselves by over-reacting to what others say or do. We have conditioned ourselves to see everyone else as "the enemy" rather than look within ourselves for the real cause of our distress.

If we can pause long enough to uncover our own hidden discomfort and distorted attitudes **before** we react with harsh criticism or vindictive silence, we can change our destructive first impulses into a loving interchange between individuals.

TODAY Let me not be quick to criticize or condemn another. I will look at others as friends, not as foes, on my journey toward self-discovery.

> "Be not angry that you cannot make others as you wish them to be since you cannot make yourself as you wish to be."
>
> —Thomas a'Kempis

> "If we could read the secret history of our enemies, we should find in each man's life sorrow and suffering enough to disarm all hostility."
>
> —Henry Wadsworth Longfellow

Let us review what others have said about listening and sharing.

"To profit from good advice requires more wisdom than to give it." —Churton Collins

They that will not be counselled cannot be helped. If you do not hear reason, she will rap you on the knuckles." —Benjamin Franklin

"Don't give your advice before you are called upon." —Erasmus

"If a man's faith is unstable and his peace of mind troubled, his knowledge will not be perfect." —Buddhist Proverb

"Let no man presume to give advice to others that he has not first lived successfully himself." —Anonymous

"People have a way of becoming what you encourage them to be—not what you nag them to be." —S.N. Parker

"An open mind, like an open window, should be screened to keep the bugs out." —Virginia Hutchinson

"Philosophy is a purely personal matter. A genuine philosopher's credo is the outcome of a single complex personality; it cannot be transferred. No two persons, if sincere, can have the same philosophy." —Havelock Ellis

TODAY I will not expect others to agree with my views. I will share and listen for what is good in others and myself. I will seek honesty and increased understanding from all my communications with others.

"I believe the purpose of my life is to learn, grow, and be the best possible person I can be," said a group member. "In order to do that, I must ask **big** questions of myself and God. I ask questions like 'What's love?' 'What's my life's work?' 'What's the best way to deal with this problem?' 'How can I best plan for the future?' 'Who and What is God?' 'What constitutes an ideal friendship or marriage?' 'What is the purpose of life?' 'What's preventing me from reaching my goal?'

"To me, asking **big** questions makes life an exciting adventure. I look upon everyone and everything as a partial answer to a larger question. Life is never boring to me. Or lonely. I treasure every experience as a means of expanding my knowledge and understanding."

TODAY I will have more questions than answers. I will ask **big** questions of God and myself. I will search for, and be receptive to, the answers to my questions in my daily experiences and endeavors.

> "It's better to ask some of the questions than to know all the answers."
>
> —James Thurber

> "Judge a man by his questions rather than his answers."
>
> —Voltaire

Chapter 12

Prayer and Guidance

The dictionary defines prayer as an "earnest request" or any "spiritual communion with God."

Many of us, when we attend meetings and earnestly share our questions and experiences, are asking for something from a Higher Power even if we do not know what that something is. The sincere desire to better our lives, and our humble attempts to seek answers to our confusions and frustrations, are nothing less than prayers in action.

Faith, according to the dictionary, is "anything believed." It is also "complete trust, confidence, and reliance" as well as "allegiance to some person or thing."

If we have placed our belief and confidence in this philosophy of living or in some of our group's members—and if we apply and act on its principles and truths, then we also have more faith than we may have given ourselves credit for. Even a minimum of faith can be used to increase our progress and the power of our prayers.

TODAY I am not so far away from God, prayer, and faith as I thought. I will reaffirm my faith in these living principles and continue my sincere desires (prayers) to improve my life.

There are as many types and forms of prayer as there are people. Some of us prefer formal prayers and rituals provided by our church; others of us, who attend no church, find comfort and inspiration in casual prayers, simply telling God what is in our minds and hearts.

It does not matter how or where we pray. What matters is that we have the willingness, and make a consistent effort, to pray. Whether our prayers express praise, thanksgiving, forgiveness, concern for a friend or stranger, or whether they contain requests for our own needs and guidance—daily contact with a Higher Power is necessary to transform our lives and to renew our courage, understanding, hope, and faith.

TODAY and EVERYDAY I will seek contact with God through formal or informal prayer. I will ask for guidance from my Higher Power to increase my strength, hope, and wisdom.

> "Pray in your own way, according to your own understanding, for God heeds and respects all languages of the human heart."

"I believe prayer and meditation," said a group member, "are two different forms of communication. In prayer, I tell God and others who I am; that is, I share what I'm grateful for and what I need help in. In meditation, I listen. That's when I allow myself to be open and receptive to all my daily experiences. Every event that happens in my life that day, every person I meet, any song I hear, any animal I see, any book I read, any child I observe are **all** messages to me from my Higher Power. I only need to stop talking and listen!

"You see, if I'm talking (praying) all the time, I won't be able to hear what God may be trying to tell me. And if I'm listening (meditating) all the time, then I can't tell God—nor do I even know myself—who **I** am. As I see it, talking and listening, prayer and meditation, giving and receiving need to be balanced if I want to have peace of mind and understanding."

TODAY I will strive for balance. If I talk too much, I will listen more. If I listen more than I speak, I will share my thoughts out loud. I can only be as close to God and others as I am to myself.

Some of us have an insatiable desire to **do** something about every situation that occurs in our lives. We fret about this, we rush into that, and we push our confused minds to the edge of despair. Weary from our relentless struggling, we become short-tempered, highly critical, and completely irrational. Little things become big things. Everything in our lives becomes too much for us.

When this happens, we need to "Let Go" of our false pride, and admit that we alone cannot understand or solve our present difficulties. Only when we have the humility to admit our limitations can we receive the help we need.

Letting go of our false pride, however, is merely the first step. We also need to "Let God" take a hand in our affairs. When we give our burdens to God expecting His help,our problems often solve themselves without our ever making any conscious effort. Leaving our troubles with God frees our minds to receive new perspectives which we could not receive while we were busily clutching our sorrows and frustrations to us.

TODAY I will ask for God's guidance and help in every area of my life. I will not try to solve all my difficulties at once. God does not expect me to handle more than my share. I will work on one or two things and leave the rest to Him.

These words were found on a cellar wall in Cologne after World War II:

"I believe in the sun
even when it is not shining;
I believe in love
even when I feel it not;
I believe in God
even when He is silent."

The author who wrote this had the kind of patience that is born of faith and courage. Despite the destruction, injustice, and fear that permeated those war years, the writer never lost faith that life, with all its apparent sorrows and seemingly senseless atrocities, was still worth living.

Can we, when faced with despair, bitterness, or grief, muster the same faith and courage? Can we still affirm, even if we do not understand or see the reasons for our misery and suffering, that there is a Higher Purpose in it, and that we shall ultimately receive the guidance and inspiration to help us overcome it?

TODAY No matter what happens, I will affirm my faith that "All is Well." I will have the courage to believe that God is guiding me, loving me, and teaching me even though I do not feel or see His presence.

Indignation, resentment, the desire to "get even" or see others punished can destroy us physically, mentally, emotionally, and spiritually. If we want to avoid the crippling effects of anger and fear, we must learn the art of prayer.

Peace of mind is gained when we repeatedly pray for those we fear or dislike by desiring for them what we wish for ourselves.

We might pray, for example, for the offending person's health, happiness, and prosperity. Some of us may only have to repeat this prayer over a period of a few days or a few weeks until our animosity leaves; others of us may need several months of persistent, daily prayer to remove more deep-seated feelings of anger, hurt, and fear.

Those of us who have sincerely tried this method of prayer—asking for others what we would ask for ourselves—can attest to its power and peace. Not only have our attitudes changed toward those who have hurt us, but quite often we have seen miraculous changes in those for whom we've prayed.

TODAY If I find myself harboring ill-will toward anyone, I will ask God to bless that person. I will pray for his or her health, happiness, and prosperity until all ill-feeling is removed.

What do I do when I earnestly pray for something and it doesn't come? Do I give up in despair? Do I doubt my faith in God? Do I stop trusting and communicating with the very source that can help me?

One of the most important things I must learn is that delay is not necessarily denial. Sometimes, God does not instantly give me what I think I need because that would not be the best thing for me or my loved ones.

Many times, I do not know what is best for me; many times, I may not be prepared to receive what I ask for. In that case, God seemingly "denies" my request in order to give me the time and opportunities to work on **becoming ready.** God then guides me in the direction I must go to improve myself so that I will benefit from my prayers.

At other times, I may be selfishly seeking fulfillment of my own needs while ignoring the needs of others. A loving God would certainly not grant my desires at the expense of another's growth and development!

TODAY I will be patient in prayer. I will not expect instant answers. I will have faith that God is working out my problems and accomplishing my desires in the best way possible for me and my loved ones.

An open mind, willingness, and faith are essential to effective prayer.

First, we must have an open mind to consider the possibility that there is a Power greater than ourselves that we can use to help us.

Second, we must have the willingness to believe that this Power hears us, loves us, and wants the best for us.

Third, we must have the faith that God **is** answering our prayers according to our best interests and growth—whether we are aware of it or not.

Only to the degree that we have an open mind, willingness, and faith can God work in us and through us. The more we develop a desire to believe and the more we strive, however clumsily or falteringly at first, to contact this Greater Power, the more we will experience unexplainable joy, harmony, and purpose in our lives. We will also begin to see the results of our prayers in numerous "coincidences" and "strange, chance events" that occur in our lives.

TODAY I will be open to the idea that there is a Power greater than myself that I can use to help me. I will have the willingness to believe that Power cares more for me than I often care for myself.

In doubting or ignoring God's willingness to act on our behalf, we often drive ourselves to the point of exhaustion and despair. We feel we must "pull ourselves up by our own bootstraps." We try, by our efforts alone, to achieve our desired goals and fail. The more we drive ourselves, the more we flounder in depression, despair, and failure—and the harder it is to exert any effort to pray or to receive God's help.

We can avoid this futile situation if we remember to pray not only in our distress, but also in our joy. A daily habit of prayer, expressing thankfulness, praise, and our desire for guidance, carries over into times of need and stress. Constant contact with God in **all** the events of our lives better prepares us to seek, and receive, guidance and wisdom should trouble or fear arise.

TODAY and EVERYDAY I will seek constant communication with God in every area and event in my life.

> "He who cannot pray when the sun is shining will not know how to pray when the clouds come."
>
> —Author Unknown

"More things are wrought by prayer than this world dreams of. . ."

—Tennyson

Although it may not be apparent to us, God answers every prayer. One of the reasons we may not recognize God's response is because we are looking for only one answer: the one we want. If we are only open to receiving what we think we need, we limit God's ability to help and guide us. And we blind ourselves to the many good gifts Our Creator wishes to give us.

The highest form of prayer is to seek God's will for us. It is only when we are fully surrendered to God's guidance and wisdom that we can truly see the real, and often far-reaching results, of prayer. To every request of ours, then, we must be careful to add such clauses as "If it be Thy will," or "According to Thy will." Such clauses at the end of our prayers admit our incomplete understanding. Surrendering to God's will also affirms our trust and faith that God will do what's best for us and those we care about.

TODAY Let me realize God answers all prayers in the best way possible. I will have the faith, humility, and open-mindedness to receive His answers. I will not expect God to answer my prayers in the way I think He should.

One source of frustration and depression comes from thinking we must take on everything at once. We think we ought to be more, do more, and resolve more than is humanly possible. Trying to analyze or solve all our confusions overnight only increases our frustration and despair. Until we "let go" of the notion that we alone are capable of handling every conflict that arises, we can make little headway in resolving any of our inner tensions.

Each of us is responsible for making the necessary efforts to better ourselves and our circumstances. But we are only **part** of the effort. Our main reliance needs to be on our Higher Power. Some conflicts and feelings take time to sort out before we can take any effective action. Letting go of those difficulties, by placing them in God's hands, is the only way to free ourselves from the overwhelming weight of feelings and confusions beyond our immediate control.

TODAY I will "Let Go and Let God" take a hand in my affairs. I know that the more I clutch my problems to me the less chance I give my Higher Power to help me. Only a calm, clear mind—free of turmoil and distress—can be receptive to answers when they do come.

Chapter 13

God and Faith

Today let us expand our concepts of God by reviewing what others throughout history have said:

"Without the assistance of (a) Divine Being. . .I cannot succeed. With that assistance, I cannot fail." —Abraham Lincoln

"The person who has a firm trust in the Supreme Being is powerful in his power, wise by his wisdom, happy by his happiness." —Joseph Addison

"Walk boldly and wisely. . .There is a hand above that will help you on." —Philip James Bailey

"What is faith unless it is to believe what you do not see?" —St. Augustine

"All who call on God in true faith, earnestly from the heart, will certainly be heard, and will receive what they have asked and desired." —Martin Luther

"All I have seen teaches me to trust the Creator for all I have not seen." —Emerson

"To them that ask, where have you seen the Gods, or how do you know for certain there are Gods, that you are so devout in their worship? I answer: Neither have I ever seen my own soul, and yet I respect and honor it." —Marcus Aurelius

TODAY I will concentrate on developing my spiritual philosophy. I will expand my ideas of faith and God by talking with others, reading, and by applying what I learn to my own life.

When the word "God" is mentioned in our meetings, it is always with the understanding that each person has his or her particular concept of that Power. So, for our purposes, "God" may be called by many names: Supreme Being, Universal Spirit, Truth, Allah, Father, Heavenly Friend, Provider, Inner Voice, Higher Power, Creative Intelligence, Merciful One, and so on.

It is not our purpose to convince anyone else that our belief, name, or concept is the **right** one. We respect each person's right to believe as he or she chooses. We believe, quite simply, that God reaches out to, and communicates with, each person in whatever way that person is capable of receiving that communication.

We also believe that God never shuts the door on anyone; it is only our willingness or unwillingness to open the door to God that permits or prevents our receiving love—just as we permit or prevent ourselves receiving love from other human beings by our open or closed responses to them.

TODAY Let me open more doors than I close by being receptive to others.

"God has many names though He is only one being."

—Aristotle

God responds to each of us according to our need. It does not matter if our concept of God differs from others' views. Nor is it important that we are not, as yet, quite clear as to what our concept of God is. What **is** important is that we think of God as supplying what we personally need.

Do we need inspiration and strength? Then God will be Enlightenment and Power. Do we need a friend? Then God will be our Companion. Are we suffering from ill-health? Then God is our Great Physician. Are we dissatisfied with work, or are we jobless? God is our Employer. When we are afraid and insecure, do we need comfort? God is Love and Assurance. Are we ashamed of our past and all our mistakes? God is Forgiveness and the Author of new beginnings.

TODAY Do I need more security, love, help, or companionship than I now possess? If so, I will ask God to be a part of my life.

> "Above all am I convinced of the need, irrevocable and inescapable, of every human heart, for God. No matter how we try to escape, to lose ourselves in restless seeking, we cannot separate ourselves from our divine source. There is no substitute for God."
>
> —A.J. Cronin

When we are filled with self-doubt, very few of us can muster the courage or confidence necessary to face even the most ordinary events. Moreover, our self-doubt often makes us question the very purpose and meaning of our lives. Although we may try to overcome our lack of self-confidence by sheer self-propulsion, too often our efforts result in exhaustion and despair. Then it is almost impossible to shut out the hundreds of additional doubts and fears that run rampant in our fatigued minds.

One sure cure for our lack of self-confidence is faith in God. For God is, after all, our Greatest Friend, Ally, and Support. Even if we can't see our way through our difficulties, God can. Quieting our minds, by affirming God's help and constant guidance, renews faith in ourselves and assures us of His loving care and protection.

TODAY I will place my faith and trust in God. I know God can do through me, and for me, what I often cannot do for myself.

> "He who has faith also has humility. He has an inward reservoir of courage, hope, confidence, calmness, an assuring trust that all will come out well—even though to the world it may appear to come out badly."
>
> —B.C. Forbes

". . .It may be that you dislike a thing, and God brings about through it a great deal of good."

—Holy Koran

Today, let us look back on our lives and discover how past, painful experiences brought growth and love into our lives. Were there times when we were lonely and frustrated? In need of a friend? What new friend came into our lives to help alleviate our loneliness?

Was there a time when "going on" seemed futile? What happened to give us renewed strength and courage? Did we join a support group? Get a raise? Find a better job? Receive a long-awaited letter? Were we surprised by an unexpected courtesy from a stranger, relative, or friend?

No matter how empty we've felt, or how low our spirits have been, help has always been available. And that same help is available today. God never fails to light our way if we can endure the darkest night. As Longfellow once wrote: "The lowest ebb is the turn of the tide."

TODAY I will review how God has loved me through my worst trials. I know that God's love is as available to me now as it was then.

"I believe self-honesty and faith are essential for a full and satisfying life," said a long-time member.

"By self-honesty I mean admitting **my** strengths and weaknesses. I don't mean, 'Let's talk about **yours!**' Self-honesty is also not talking about the way I **was,** but the way I **am.** Self-honesty means I may have come a long way, but I'm still nowhere near the perfection I desire. Self-honesty means I'm still struggling like the rest of you, that I don't have all the answers for you **or** myself, and that growing and changing are forever.

"Faith in a Higher Power is also a must for me. I've seen God perform a lot of miracles in my life when I was sure I had no strength to carry on. That's true even now. I really believe the saying, 'With God, nothing is impossible.' As long as I keep my heart pure, in self-honesty and faith in action, I can endure and overcome anything."

TODAY By placing my faith in self-honesty and God, I will have a rich and full life.

> "A humble knowledge of oneself is a surer road to God than a deep searching of the sciences."
>
> —Thomas a'Kempis

We must be careful, once we have accepted the Higher Power concept of this living philosophy, not to make our individual faith an escape from reality. In other words, we should not ask God to do for us what we can do for ourselves.

Faith is not false security nor a convenient crutch to help us avoid troublesome problems or irksome responsibilities. True faith is a reliance on God to show us the best decision to make and the best direction to take—often in the face of obstacles. We do not expect God to do all the work, and magically remove our difficulties, while we rest on previous victories or remain passively pious. Relief and answers come only to the extent that we are willing to make concerted efforts to change our own attitudes and actions. In order to discover what we can or cannot change in our lives, we must be open to God's guidance and wisdom.

TODAY I will not make my reliance on God an excuse not to do my part. I will wait for God's direction with an open mind and an eager heart.

> "This is what I found out about religion: it gives you courage to make the decisions you must make in a crisis and the confidence to leave the results to a higher Power. Only by trust in God can a man carrying responsibility find repose."
>
> —Dwight D. Eisenhower

If we have been hurt or disappointed by significant people in our lives, we may find it difficult, at first, to trust in God. If we wish to receive the full benefits of God's loving help and guidance, we must break down our fear-filled barriers by making whatever effort we can to trust. Distrust and doubt can only limit God's power to help us.

But how, we may ask, can we begin to trust again? Especially when we have so many painful and disillusioning memories? Our first step is to **replace** our negative fears with more knowledge of God.

To begin with, God is **not** like the possessive, punishing, or fear-filled people we've known. God does not want to limit our freedom as much as give it to us. God wants us to experience joy, inner peace, and wholeness. God wishes us to be partners with Him—not adversaries or slaves. Furthermore, God will never ask us to sacrifice anything that is vitally important to our physical, mental, emotional, or spiritual well-being.

TODAY I will not base my faith and trust in God on my negative experiences with others. I will dare to believe God is wiser, more loving, and more powerful than anyone I have ever known. I will also believe God is willing to supply me with what I personally need for my best growth.

"Experience is not what happens to you;
it is what you **do** with what happens to you."

—Aldous Huxley

I can aggravate or alleviate many of my difficulties by the way I react to them. Exaggerating the seriousness of my experiences may indicate I am more comfortable with misery than inner contentment. Such distortions of reality create innumerable excuses for continued failure and often disguise my lack of desire to change.

If, on the other hand, I react calmly to my situation, I free my mind to think more clearly and rationally. A mind free from anxiety and fear can be filled with affirmations of God's guidance, protection, and goodness. Facing difficulties with calm assurance that good will prevail gives me courage, hope, and faith. I can then respond to my experiences secure in the knowledge that I will be guided to right decisions and new perspectives.

TODAY I will not over-react to my experiences. I will replace fear with faith. I will reaffirm God's guidance, protection, and love in my life no matter what happens.

Is God "our refuge and strength, a very present help in trouble," or is alcohol, drugs, over-activity, work, cigarettes, peer approval, and food?

Do we try to fill our thirst for more knowledge of, and faith in, God with remedies which anesthetize—not revitalize—us? Do we over-exert ourselves in activities, drown ourselves in work's problems and routines, saturate ourselves with social gatherings to avoid coming to terms with our inner anxieties, fears, and self-doubts? Do we rely on food or entertainment to satisfy the hunger of our spirits—when the real issue is our need for more insight, understanding, and faith?

If we continue to apply self-will to our problems rather than seek the strength and guidance of a Higher Authority, we will continue to feel empty, frustrated, and fatigued.

TODAY I will turn to God in my emptiness and frustration. I will ask for more understanding, faith, and guidance in my daily life.

> "Man is a peculiar, puzzling paradox, groping for God and hoping to hide from Him at the selfsame time."
>
> —Dr. William Arthur Ward

Sometimes we find ourselves completely overwhelmed by our circumstances or our confusing thoughts and feelings. When we feel crushed by the weight of it all, what can we do? The best solution is to turn our lives over to the care of God, asking only for His will to be done.

When we seek God's will and direction, we open the door to a Power greater than our own. We place our burdens on someone's shoulders Who can bear the weight. We admit that we are not strong enough to carry the tremendous load we thought it was our responsibility to bear. And we surrender to the fact that we do not have sufficient knowledge or understanding to resolve our quandaries alone.

Abraham Lincoln found tremendous power and peace in surrendering his will to God's will. Lincoln stated: "I have had so many evidences of God's direction . . .that I cannot doubt that this power comes from God. I frequently see my way clear to a decision when I am conscious that I have not sufficient facts on which to found it. I am satisfied that, when the Almighty wants me to do, or not to do, a particular thing, He finds a way of letting me know."

TODAY I will take my cares to God. I am confident God will lighten my confusion and suggest the right way for me to go.